The Colour

Green

Amanda Ellieson

This book is dedicated to the people who
brought a dream to life.
Through their positivity, people have inspired
and encouraged.
To the people who believed in our son when it
mattered the most.
We thank you and salute you.

CONTENTS

INTRODUCTION

Before I begin, I feel it would be beneficial to the reader to have some knowledge of the Royal Marine Corps. They are, to most, an enigma. We rarely see or hear any of the excellent work they carry out, from guardians of the UK's nuclear deterrents to completing drug busts in the Gulf. They also carry out many humanitarian deployments. For instance, in the wake of the Beirut explosion, a protection team from 42 Commando was deployed with HMS Enterprise. This team was sent to support the UK's efforts following the explosion, which devastated Lebanon's capital city.

They will no doubt continue to hide their light under a bushel for many years to come.

The Royal Marines Commandos are the sea soldiers of the Royal Navy. Their motto 'Per Mare, Per Terram' means 'By sea, By Land'. The Latin phrase symbolises the Royal Marines' dual role as an elite amphibious fighting force, operating onboard ships and ashore. They are a highly specialised and adaptable light infantry force.

The Corps has a proud history and unique traditions. Their colours (flags) do not carry individual battle honours in the manner the British Army does but rather the 'Great Globe Itself' as the symbol of the Corps. King George IV chose the Great Globe surrounded by laurels as a symbol of the Marines' successes in every quarter of the world.

They are also known as Royals, Bootys, The Corps, Leathernecks or Bootnecks. The latter name derives from the early days of the marines when they belonged to the Duke of York and Albany's Regiment of Foot, which was formed in 1664. As they waded to shore, the lads removed their unpractical boots and put their rounds and powder in them. The most recent adaptation of why they are called 'Bootnecks' or 'Leathernecks' is derived from the leather that Marines used to cut from their boots and wrap around their necks to stop their throats from being cut. I am sure there are many more stories regarding the word used for a Royal Marine.

The ethos of commitment, teamwork, and loyalty, combined with the commando spirit, is indicative of a Royal Marine, and that will never change.

The four elements of the commando spirit are; courage, determination, unselfishness, and cheerfulness in the face of adversity, which is well known to all in the Corps. The Corps operates in all environments and climates. They offer expertise and training in amphibious warfare, arctic and mountain warfare, and expeditionary warfare. Additionally, it demonstrates a substantial commitment to the United Kingdom Rapid Reaction Forces.

Throughout its 356 year history, the Royal Marines have seen action in several significant wars, often fighting alongside the British Army. The Corps has mainly been deployed in expeditionary warfare roles during the Falklands War, the Gulf war, Bosnia, Kosovo, the Sierra Leone civil war, and Iraq and Afghanistan. The Royal Marines have close international ties with allied marine forces, particularly the United States Marine Corps and the Netherlands Marine Corps.

Today, the Royal Marines are an elite fighting force within the British Armed Forces, having undergone many substantial changes over time.

One of these changes took place in April 2017 when the First Sea Lord Admiral, Sir Philip Jones, announced that the Royal Marines would be restructured. A Future Commando Force (FCF) has been set up under Naval Command to create the staff and intellectual horsepower for a land littoral strike division.

The Royal Marine must undergo one of the most extended and most physically demanding training regimes globally.

Recruit training lasts 32 weeks, and potential recruits must be aged between 16 and 32 years old. The potential recruit must undergo interviews, medical tests, psychometric tests, and a pre-joining fitness test. Once the individual passes all the above, he must take a three-day selection course called a PRMC (Pre Royal Marine Course). This takes place at Commando Training Centre, Lympstone, Devon. Upon passing the course, the recruit will then start basic training.

The recruit will learn and develop military skills throughout basic training. These skills include weapons handling, marksmanship, proficiency with different firearms, marching and parade ground skills, map reading and navigation, physical fitness, and mental toughness.

They also learn about fieldcraft, such as camouflage and stalking, basic survival skills, patrolling, and sentry duty development. Unarmed and armed close-quarter combat is also taught alongside first aid and underwater escape. Chemical, biological and radiological nuclear training is given. Military communications and signals, amphibious landings training, and teamwork skills all play a part in the training of a Royal Marine.

While on the course, recruits undergo continuous testing. Failure to pass a given test twice will result in a back troop. The recruit will retrain and be given another opportunity with a new troop to pass.

As training comes to a close, the recruit is expected to complete four commando tests. The first one being an endurance course, the second a nine-mile speed march, the third a Tarzan assault course, and lastly, a 30-mile speed march across upland Dartmoor. After the 30-mile speed march across Dartmoor, anyone who has failed any of the tests may attempt to retake them up until the seven-day window expires. Until they have passed the tests, no one is regarded as a Royal Marine Commando and will not be awarded the coveted green beret. The recruits in their final week of training are known as Kings Squad. This is a tradition that has been in place since His Majesty King George V granted the honour in 1918.

The most outstanding recruit from a troop will be awarded a King's badge. King George the V directed that his Royal Cipher, surrounded by the laurel wreath, would be known as the King's badge. The King's Badge award is an accolade for the most outstanding overall recruit during training. The King's badge recipient is chosen from among the diamonds. Diamonds are recruits who hold command responsibilities within the troop and will have leadership roles when on exercise.

After passing out, the Royal Marine will leave the training centre to take up his post as a Marine in one of the six units. He will carry out general duties for an average of two years before specialising in a specific role.

There are only 7200 Royal Marines in the world, and they are scattered around the globe, in comparison to the British Army, which stands at 112,000 soldiers.

In my opinion, this figure illustrates how small and exclusive the Royal Marine family is within the Royal Navy. To be a member, you would need to have that 'state of mind'.

THE ROYAL MARINES DICTIONARY

As you start reading, the Corps' 356-year history, commandos, or bootnecks, as they are affectionately known, have established customs and traditions of their own, along with some intriguing vocabulary to match.

Many of these phrases have slipped into everyday language, while others leave us civvies scratching our heads, feeling baffled.

Here are some examples of the Royal Marine Dictionary Dan uses all the time, which his father and I unintentionally have picked up:

- Brammer - outstandingly good
- Icers or redders - something very cold or very hot
- Zap/Zapped - to shoot or be shot at
- Stickies - cake
- Common Dog - common sense
- Trap - to successfully attract a member of the opposite sex
- Donkey Wallopers - The cavalry
- Gonk – Sleep

- Church Key - a device equipped with both a bottle and can opener
- Glophead - a habitual drunkard
- Laughing Kitbags - to find something funny
- Heads - toilets
- Banjo - broken or broken down
- Waz/wazzer – fantastic
- Oppo - a close friend
- Zeds - sleep
- Sneaky Beaky - intelligence staff
- Sweating neaters - to be worried
- Rug rat - a baby
- Hoofing - brilliant
- Threaders - awful
- Scran - food
- Honkin - awful.
- Goppin' – disgusting
- Gen - really
- Essence - good looking
- Spinning - telling a story
- Hoggin - water

- Grotts – accommodation

BEDTIME STORIES

How did this adventure begin, I hear people say? The answer to that lies in the pages you are about to turn. Parents can influence their children in many ways without even knowing it. Without direction, there is no journey. Without a journey, there is no story.

Daniel had jumped on the sofa next to his father. Jon put his arm around the young boy and pulled him close. It was nearly bedtime, and Daniel knew his father would carry him upstairs in just a few more minutes. They both would snuggle down on Daniel's bed, and Jon would read another chapter from his storybook.

I had walked into the lounge just as an advert from a famous travel company had finished. It was apparent the advert had caught Daniel's eye. He was asking his dad if they could visit there on holiday. Jon told his charge we wouldn't be able to afford it, but perhaps they could find out about the pirate ship while out shopping on Saturday.

Jon scooped his son up and made their way upstairs. His voice could soon be heard reading a story to his son.

Later that evening the advert made a repeat performance. Jon explained Daniel had been mesmerised by the pirate ship in the swimming pool. His two favourite things were swimming and pirate ships. They had recently watched Pirates of the Caribbean, so he had become obsessed with pirates, and Jon took Dan swimming each weekend.

On Saturday, the boys came back with a glossy holiday brochure. The pirate ship in the swimming pool was an all-inclusive holiday in Benalmadena, Spain. Daniel was so excited to show me the pictures of the resort and its many child-friendly attractions. The price was something else. I only worked part-time, and there wasn't much spare money at the end of each month after paying all the bills, especially not for a luxurious holiday.

Over the next couple of weeks, the pirate ship became the hot topic of conversation. Each time we switched the television on as if by magic, the advert would appear.

Jon worked as a maintenance engineer at the local brewery. He had been there for many years and enjoyed the versatile role he did. Jon had recently worked overtime on his days off. He came in exhausted one evening from work. As soon as Jon sat down, Daniel climbed onto his knee and snuggled up with him before heading to bed.

I was finishing Jon's tea off when the kitchen door burst open. Daniel stood with his father and announced we were off to see the pirate ship. He was so excited, proclaiming it would be the best holiday ever.

Each evening we would now be watching out for the advert. When it came on, Daniel would describe all the games he and his dad would play on the pirate ship.

Jon had explained that if we were careful with our spare cash and he worked some more overtime, we would be able to afford it. So Daniel came with us to the travel agents and explained to the lady organising the trip that he was taking us to see the pirate ship. She thought this was hilarious, and although only six years old, there were plenty of things for him to do in Benalmadena. Including a kids club, which would be beneficial in more ways than one. Everybody from the postman to the dinner lady at school knew we were off to see the pirate ship.

The months flew by, and the holiday drew ever closer. We had decided not to tell Daniel what day we would fly out to Spain because none of us would get any sleep running up to our departure. The morning we were due to leave, we woke Dan up early. It was still dark outside, and he couldn't quite get to grips with what was going on. Dad whispered in his ear our intentions. He shot out of bed, running onto the landing in disbelief. He hurriedly packed some toys, then had some breakfast, chattering all the while.

The taxi was waiting for us outside. Jon loaded the suitcases into the boot, and we were off. We had never been on an all-inclusive holiday before, so it would also be a treat for Jon and me. Daniel had never been on an aeroplane, so this journey was destined to be huge for our little boy.

We found our designated seats on the plane. Daniel persuaded his dad he should have the window seat because he was the youngest. As the plane roared along the runway, Daniel held on tight to his dad's hand. You could see the colour draining from his face. Slowly the plane lifted from the runway, and before we knew it, we were in the clouds. The colour soon returned to Dan's face, and he talked about the imminent landing with his dad whilst tucking into his lunch.

The plane landed on time. The heat was overwhelming as we walked down the steps of the plane. We were ushered onto an air-conditioned coach, which took us straight to the resort. As the coach made its way up to the resort, we could see the many swimming pools and activities being used. The resort was huge, and Daniel was beyond happy. He had already told his dad the first thing they would do when we had unpacked was to set out in search of the infamous pirate ship.

We were warmly greeted and given a key card for our room. Our room was on the first floor, so we found it and opened the door. The room was beyond our expectations, Jon and I started to unpack, and Daniel had his suitcase open and was eagerly looking for his swimming shorts while persuading his father to get ready as well.

We all left the hotel room together; we had been given a map of the resort. Daniel had worked out the ship was across the road in the other part of the resort.

So, with beach towels in hand, we crossed the busy road using the footbridge, up a few steps and through the small bar area.

Daniel ran towards the pirate ship. He could just about make out the flag which sat on the crow's nest, which he had seen so many times on the advert.

We could see the pirate ship; it was right in front of us; Jon and I looked across, gobsmacked. The pirate ship had an out-of-order sign on it.

Daniel was in the water, heading right for it. Jon followed him in to try and explain he would be unable to climb on it. I had never seen Daniel so distraught; the tears rolled down his face. It was heartbreaking to watch. Finally, Jon calmed him down and took him to look at the water rapids ride on the other side of the resort.

As they returned, I could see Jon and Daniel walking towards me. Daniel was still upset about the pirate ship, so Jon sat him down on one of the sunbeds in the shade and began to tell him a story about the jungle. Daniel slowly drifted off to sleep, and peace was restored.

Daniel woke up sometime later and wanted to see if the pirate ship was still out of order. Jon took him back to the pool where the ship lay. The sign was still up, and nothing had changed. So, they discussed their next move—nothing else for it: the ice cream hut. Jon plied him with ice cream, and for the time being, the pirate ship was forgotten.

That evening we ate in the main restaurant; Daniel wandered around the buffet with his father filling his plate; he got impatient as he knew the kid's show was about to start, and he desperately wanted to meet his newfound friends.

So, as a way of amusing him while we enjoyed our meal, Jon would share secrets of when he was a 'special agent in the jungle'. Daniel fell for the stories hook line and sinker. Each evening Jon would make a story up to keep Daniel amused. Some of the stories were quite explicit. Jon would be dropped into the jungle by helicopter to find the baddie. He would wrestle with crocodiles and use the wildebeest to travel on to his destinations. Daniel listened to every word his father was spinning him.

Some of the stories or 'missions', as he called them, were so outlandish, yet Daniel loved to hear them. Of course, it kept him occupied while we enjoyed our meal.

The pirate ship remained closed during our visit. Apparently, some of the wood under the water needed replacing due to its unsafe condition. I must admit, Daniel would visit the pirate ship each day. However, as the days passed and it remained closed, he accepted he would not be playing on it anytime soon. His dream of playing on the pirate ship had diminished. As a result, he realised that some things are beyond our control. We can't change them, so there is no point in dwelling on them. Move on. (He still has that attitude today).

All too soon, it was time to leave the resort and return to reality. We all enjoyed the holiday and vowed to return one day.

The stories Jon told Daniel came back with us too. For a while, Daniel refused to have his nightly story. He wanted to listen to another mission Jon had undertaken as a secret agent. Seemingly, Daddy did lots of undetected work for the government as well.

One particular day I was standing in the playground waiting for Daniel to finish school. I could see him putting his little green blazer on and his cap and grabbing his satchel.

The lady who was standing next to me had made conversation many times before. Her son was in the same class as Daniel. This conversation started as a whisper; she explained she hadn't realised Jon worked for the government and the dangerous job he did. If I ever needed any assistance with Daniel while Jon was away, I should not hesitate to ask for her help.

I did not know where to put myself; I hoped the ground would swallow me up. The awful thing was I just nodded and thanked the lady for the kind gesture. We parted at that point as the children ran towards us. I didn't want to mention the conversation to Daniel until I had spoken to our very own special agent.

When I explained to Jon what had happened in the playground that afternoon, he was in hysterics. Thinking about it when I returned home, I had made the situation worse by agreeing with her when I should have put the poor lady straight (if you are that lady reading this book, I'm so sorry).

Daniel had obviously spoken to her little boy and shared that his dad was a special agent.

So Jon's stories about his younger days as a uncover spy had dropped us well and truly in it. Daniel must have believed Jon was a special agent, and what made it worse was the new 007 movie had just come out. So to a little boy with a big imagination, it was all entirely believable.

I remember Jon had even taken him to the toy shop to get the 'all singing and dancing' gadget pen Daniel Craig used in the movie; we had to sit through hours of 007 movies at the weekends.

We decided to break the news to Daniel gently that he wasn't the son of a special agent.

Jon tried numerous times but to no avail. He said he wouldn't tell anybody else, and his secret was safe with him.

As a result, we decided to leave the subject and hoped it would run its course. The special agent stories came to a close, but adventure stories took their place. Jon would take him on journeys up Mount Everest through his imagination. Daniel would point out to his father that he would climb that mountain one day, and I have no doubt he will. They would abseil down cliff faces, swim through frozen lakes. All through the power of the spoken word.

Daniel grew up with a thirst for knowledge and a desire to experience. So his birthday parties as a young boy were not the usual kind of party - Gorging in Yorkshire, Aerial Extreme and Ninja Warrior in Manchester, but to name a few.

We encouraged him to try new things, to do things most boys would think were dangerous. "It's only dangerous if you don't know what you are doing, Mum," he would say (he still says it, although it has more meaning now).

His father and I have, indirectly, given him the most significant gift of all. The knowledge that you can accomplish anything if you have a passion and drive for it. Daniel has been inspired to grasp life through Jon's stories and my constant encouragement to be the best version of himself he can be. In order to make a difference, we've always attempted to steer him away from the majority and head towards the minority. It will undoubtedly be a harder path to follow but more rewarding at the end of it.

THE BEGINNING OF A DREAM

Daniel was fourteen. We were in the throes of starting to think about his future and which direction he wanted to concentrate. His teachers suggested A levels, and the world could be his oyster, whether an apprenticeship or college. Dan had struggled with dyslexia from an early age. Having had recent tests, the school decided it would be in Dan's best interest to apply for a twenty-minute extension time to his exams. In addition, they applied for a reader, which, inevitably, would make his life easier.

For Dan, the thought of carrying on full-time education did not appeal whatsoever. He had always been more practical than academic. Although a clever lad, he struggled putting pen to paper.

We had the conversations, but I seemed to feel he was holding back and had other ideas.

Eventually, it all came tumbling out one evening during a meal. Dan wanted to be a Royal Marine Commando. He knew all there was to know about the Royal Marines; the one thing he didn't realise was how difficult it was going to be. I didn't take the conversation too seriously. Dan was young, so the likelihood of him changing his mind was high.

We decided to take him to an Armed Forces Recruitment Centre. Neither Jon nor I knew very much about the Royal Marines, who were attached to the Royal Navy, so it would be an education for all three of us. I made the appointment, and at the time, I felt pretty confident we could put this idea firmly in the past. How wrong was I?

A young man in uniform greeted us with a huge smile. He introduced himself as Officer Shaw and gave us a brief background of his career up to press. During the conversation, we explained that we were on a fact-finding mission.

Dan showed an eagerness I had not seen in him before. His eyes lit up, and he hung onto every word Officer Shaw said. Dan asked every question known to man, from basic training to Special Forces. The main question that sticks in my mind is, "What do I need to do to be considered for a place on the training course to be a Royal Marine?"

The list was endless and, at that moment, seemed way too complicated, both mentally and physically, for my skinny little mite of a son to even consider.

The words that kept reverberating in my head were 'only one in one hundred' gets through the gruelling 32-week course. Dan had heard this but kept asking questions while at the same time keeping his eyes firmly on the person giving him the information.

With all the answers firmly imprinted on our minds, a handful of brochures, and a promise to return one year later, we left.

I needed to digest what had been discussed. Nevertheless, I still felt a glimmer of hope that Dan would make a less dangerous career choice, and I wouldn't have to give parenthood up just yet.

Jon seemed to take it in his stride. His son was aiming for the stars, and he was very proud of him for that at such a young age.

For the next twelve months, Dan's life changed considerably. While preparing to sit his GCSEs the following year, he started a fitness regime like no other. He was up at 5.30 am each morning, interval training, long-distance running, press-ups, push-ups, sit-ups. You name it; he did it. The deciding factor that this career choice was here to stay was when he started eating vegetables and having protein shakes full of fruit.

We embarked on various trips. One was down to Portsmouth to see the Docks and, of course, the Royal Marine Museum. It became apparent that The Royal Marines were no ordinary fighting force; they are an elite force, trained to be the finest in the world and a genuine Band of Brothers for life. The enthusiasm Dan showed throughout our visit was so surprising. We travelled to the submarine museum by boat, where he picked up information about The Cockleshell Heroes. Dan was amazed at the information he picked up about the 10 Royal Marines, who in December 1942 went on a secret mission so daring and dramatic they were hailed as heroes. Unbeknown to them, when they signed up for 'hazardous service', their job was to attack enemy German ships moored at the port of Bordeaux in occupied France from their canoes.

Only two marines survived to tell the story of the raid. Winston Churchill reportedly claimed that the Royal

Marines' bravery on that December evening had, in effect, shortened the war by six months. The story was later made into a film.

The new aircraft carrier Queen Elizabeth could be seen in the docks. I couldn't believe how vast it was in the flesh and imagined Dan being stationed on it in the future.

While travelling home on the train, we spoke about Dan's possibility of making such a journey, changing trains in London, etc. In any case, I knew if this was ever to be comfortable for me, I would have to make sure he had the tools of a man, not a boy.

Our next trip took place between Christmas and New Year. Jon's jaw dropped to the floor when I informed him we were off to Amsterdam for a couple of days. I know what you are thinking, and no, it was not that kind of trip. Dan was fifteen, and I wanted him to see the outside world as it looked to other people and walk along the canal banks looking at ladies of the night. Knowing what a sex show was about (which incidentally Jon took great pleasure in introducing him to, may I add). I needed Dan to have a 'been there, done that' kind of attitude, which is part of the growing up process. I was trying to accelerate this so he wouldn't be out of his depth on a social scale.

I must admit we had fun. We roared with laughter in certain situations. I will never forget the five-legged elephant and nearly being run over by a dutchman on a bicycle travelling at speed. The city is vibrant and full of culture. The famous Albert Cuyp Market was located near our accommodation. In the morning, the smell of freshly baked bread filled our flat from the many stalls on the market. Every day on our way to the city, we walked through it, watching people interact with the stall owners. Even in December, tulips could be bought from the many stalls in an array of stunning colours.

In addition to the Zoo, we visited the Holocaust museum on the outskirts of the city. A knowledgeable morning with regard to history and the ravages of war, but also filled with sadness at the countless lives lost. We spent New Year's Eve in Dam square watching the many people randomly letting off fireworks. There were street entertainers from all walks of life performing, and the atmosphere was electric. A very apt place to spend

New Year in what was going to be a very challenging year ahead. We flew from Schiphol airport the following day, having had a fantastic three-day break in an outstanding city.

We returned home and back to the grindstone. I knew this year was destined to be a game-changer for Dan, and we needed to be on hand to support him through it.

During this time, I began to think about our life without Dan in it; the very thought reduced me to a blubbering wreck. He was so young, so vulnerable, so naive in the way the world turned each day. My thoughts shifted into overdrive late in the evenings. I would sink my face into a pillow so Dan wouldn't hear me crying, in the next bedroom, over what was about to happen. I knew I needed to allow him to move on, but I wasn't ready to do it just yet.

Exactly one year later, we returned to see Officer Shaw in February. He recognized Dan straight away and couldn't quite believe how much he had changed. He had grown both in length and width and looked mature for his years.

He explained the application process and when he would be old enough to apply. Officer Shaw also walked us through all the stages step by step. Dan would have to pass each stage to get a place on the (PRMC) Pre Royal Marine Course, a three-day endurance test at the training centre at Lympstone in Devon.

I awoke early on the 17th of March 2019 to tapping computer keys, and I knew who the culprit was and why. Dan was 15 years and nine months old. He was now eligible to apply to become a Royal Marine. We went through the application to make sure he had filled everything in and let him press the send key, all the while my stomach was doing somersaults.

Within a couple of days, we were swamped with paperwork, security clearances, medical forms. We muddled through those and started to arrange appointments. The first being the eye test which he passed. The next was a medical; he had to be a certain weight, 65kg and above. At the most, Dan weighed 63kg, so he was 2kg short of the required weight. He was probably eating five decent meals a day and burning that off with his training. The decision was taken to fill

Dan with two litres of water before entering the medical centre. Nervously, he stepped on the scales, and to his surprise, he now weighed 65kg. A pass all around. He came out crossed-legged but happy.

While Dan attended high school, he had appointments during school hours. The school's pastoral coordinator, made everything so easy for us. I gave her the dates that Dan needed to be absent from school, and she arranged everything from the school's perspective. Jon or I would pick him up from school looking smart in his green blazer. We would whisk him wherever he needed to be and then back to school. We were lucky that both the school and the recruitment centre did their utmost to complete the tasks required before Dan sat his GCSE exams. We also had to make time for Dan to attend interviews for apprenticeships in Engineering as a fallback if his dream fell through.

Psychometric tests had been discussed, and I must admit, I did not know much about them. So we used Google to find the answers we needed. We ordered Dan the Royal Navy Psychometric test book. He completed ten questions of varying difficulty in the time allotted and revised for his exams each evening. We continued this until the day came to sit the actual tests.

Dan had to complete his tests at the Recruitment centre. We knew this would be a big ask because he struggled with reading as part of his dyslexia. His dad, Jon, dropped him off then waited pensively for the result. The longer he was in there, the better the chances of a pass.

In the recruitment centre, Dan was ushered into a room with twenty other candidates. He sat at a desk, and when told, he turned the first paper over. Each test paper was against the clock, and when finished, the test papers were collected to be marked. The person leading the tests would then return. He called out specific candidates' names. They would then leave the room, never to be seen again. Jon had his eyes fixed on the door to the centre. Each time the door opened, Jon's heart was in his throat, hoping he didn't see his son's face amongst the unhappy bunch exiting the building. Finally, there were just three candidates left when the last test paper was taken. One of those was Dan. An impressive 82% pass.

The next appointment we made was at a local gym; Dan had to complete two runs on a treadmill. The first was a 1.5 mile run on a 2% incline in 12.30 minutes with a thirty-second rest. Then the second run of 1.5 miles in under 10.30 minutes.

Jon once more drove him to the appointment and walked into the gym reception with Dan. They ushered him upstairs into the lion's den. Dan's blood pressure was taken before the start of the run; it was a little high, so they repeated the test once more, and as it had come down considerably, he was able to start. The instructor pointed out that it wasn't unusual for it to be high; it was probably due to nerves. Jon sat in the reception area with fingers and toes crossed and his stomach-churning. The next thing, the instructor came rushing down the stairs and asked Jon to follow him as there was a problem.

Jon took a deep breath and followed him upstairs. Dan was in tears and inconsolable.

As it turned out, the first run was perfect and well within the time. Dan approached the last 500 metres mark on the second run and decided to turn the treadmill up. Unfortunately, he pressed the stop button. A massive big fat fail.

Dan would now have to wait another three months to re-take the tests. Jon and Dan arrived home. The moment he walked through the front door, I could see Dan's tearful face. It was not going to be good news. He was distraught and annoyed with himself. I put my natural feelings of wanting to hug him and tell him everything would be okay aside and launched myself into a torrent of 'man up' verbalisation. I told him he would have to accept it and move on. My lecture ultimately did the trick. It was a lesson learned on how to deal with failure, pick yourself up, repeat, repeat, repeat until you get it right.

The instructor rang the recruitment centre and explained what had happened, and they agreed he could redo the test. The gym manager was kind enough to give Dan a pass so he could familiarise himself with the treadmill and re-do the test when he felt comfortable. Jon took him to the gym several times over the following week. Soon he became proficient at using the treadmill. A lady who used the gym regularly commented on his running style and how it seemed effortless. This small gesture made such a difference to Dan's confidence. Now he was ready to take the test.

A couple of days later, Dan retook the test and passed.

The interview was next. Dan was pretty confident in his approach to this next step. The school had been proactive in its approach to giving students training, from dress code to answering questions assertively. He had also gained some experience of this when applying for apprenticeships. His strategy had worked as he had secured himself a three-year engineering apprenticeship at a prestigious local engineering company. So, after practising a few classic interview questions, he donned his finest bib and tucker and set off again with Jon by his side. This was the final hurdle to jump to secure a place on the Pre Royal Marine Course.

When the clock struck eleven, I knew he would be in the thick of it. At the age of fifteen, Dan was sitting in an interview trying to convince somebody of his worth. At that point, I wanted him to succeed more than anything. I was mentally willing him on and praying all would turn out well for him.

I heard the car reverse onto the drive. This was it, the moment I had been dreading. Either way, this was bound to hurt. I braced myself. He came through the front door with a massive smirk on his face and a look of sheer joy. It took me all my strength to control the tears rolling down my cheeks. He had passed everything. Now he would be invited down to Lympstone to do his Pre Royal Marines three-day course.

Both Jon and I were so proud of him. It was a remarkable achievement to get this far. If Dan had failed any of these tests, particularly the academic ones, he would be able to retake them. However, he would have to wait three months for the opportunity to come round again.

Dan received a letter the following week with a kit list and the three-day program. He could now concentrate on his GCSE exams and give them 100%.

His discipline in organising his time for revision was exceptional. Not once did I ever say, "have you done your revision?" Dan was either at a revision session organised by the school or had his head in a file soaking up all the information.

The drive for this was he required at least 5 GCSE passes to be offered a place on the Royal Marine 32 week training course. One was English, and the other was mathematics; English language and English literature were his weakest subjects due to his dyslexia. His English teacher had organised extra revision sessions, which Dan attended regularly.

In his downtime, he spent hours in the school gym perfecting his running. To prepare for the Royal Marine bleep test, he would complete a rigorous workout every night. This test was found online while scouring the internet for any information regarding his chosen career path. Jon had installed a pull-up bar which was the only piece of equipment he needed to complete his workout. Every exercise he performed was done to perfection. We were required to lie on the floor with a hand underneath his chest for push-ups to make sure he was low enough, and as his body tired, he didn't arch his back. For sit-ups, we had to hold his feet down. To meet all the requirements, he must complete a minimum number of each exercise. Dan wasn't interested in just passing; he wanted to excel in each exercise. Everything he did, he completed perfectly. The pull-ups were the most difficult. When we initially installed the pull-up bar, the benchmark for a pass was five. By the time Dan made it to Lympstone, he could do double the required pull-ups easily.

LOOKING TO THE FUTURE

We, as a family, began to look at the future. It was apparent by now that Daniel was determined to achieve his dream. He certainly wasn't about to give up on this even if he failed the three-day course. He would keep trying until he succeeded. So it was more of a case of when not if.

I had spent the last fifteen years considering somebody else's needs before my own. Jon had worked shift work, two days and two nights for the previous twenty years, so getting to grips with the thought that Dan was leaving the nest and starting a new life, I realised that I would not only have a lot of free time on my hands, but I would also spend a lot of it on my own.

We decided a new member of the family would be most agreeable. It would solve the excess time I would have on my hands and cure the loneliness I would undoubtedly face from time to time.

Yes, we decided to get a puppy. A beautiful chocolate Labrador called Ellie.

Dan had no idea we were even considering it. He walked in from school one day to see this small chocolate bundle heading towards him. Dan had always wanted a puppy and had admired the Labrador breed from afar. The two of them formed an unbreakable bond from that very moment. Ellie would follow Dan everywhere. He would sit cross-legged on the floor, and Ellie would climb up and snuggle down while he continued revising. She would pinch his socks and tease him, running around the house. Ellie would hide behind the settee waiting for Dan to rearrange the lounge furniture to catch her out. He would no sooner have retrieved his sock, turned to return upstairs, and she would be running past him on the stairs and into the garden with his undies. Before too long, most of Dan's socks and underwear had tiny holes where Ellie had sank her teeth into the material.

We also covered for Ellie on occasion. She was only twelve weeks old and teething when she decided to redesign the skirting boards in the kitchen. Ellie also took a chunk out of the wall by the back door. What a mess. Dan sanded down the skirting boards while I drove to the local pet store; I wanted to buy her a crate for when we were at work and school.

We managed to restore normality to the kitchen between the two of us before Jon came home to the skirting boards looking decidedly white and the puppy looking sweet and innocent in her new bed.

He smelt a rat straight away but didn't seem overly concerned, probably because he was also finding Ellie irresistible too.

Dan finished his last exam on Friday, the 14th of June. On the following Monday, he would start his apprenticeship. It also was Dan's 16th birthday. He had officially left school and was beginning a work-based course in engineering—another tick.

Dan woke early on Monday morning; he'd had his sixteenth birthday get-together with his friends and family the day before. We had decided to splash out for his sixteenth birthday and bought him the Canada Goose jacket he had been admiring for some time. Having opened his presents, he completed his exercise routine, showered, and was ready for his first day at work.

It was unbelievable to think he was starting work and earning his own money. I dropped him off in front of a sizeable, intimidating building, and with his packed lunch in hand and a word of encouragement, he followed a group of employees indoors.

I picked him up on my way home from work. He had decided to make use of the employee facilities. The company had built a fantastic gym, and it was one of the many perks of the job. He had three weeks before he set out on his three-day PRMC, so as each day passed, he upped the ante with his exercise.

Dan's school had arranged a prom evening for all the leavers in Dan's year. It was at a local hotel called the The Grand. There was much conversation about how the guests would arrive; some parents arranged limousines or hired sports cars for the evening, others picked tractors and quad bikes. Parents waited for their children to arrive in their chosen vehicles. Dan and Cameron, his partner in crime, sped down the long sweeping drive on two mobility scooters tucked behind a Rolls Royce, taking a princess to the ball. As the Rolls Royce slowed down, Dan and Cameron accelerated, pushing the mobility scooters to the limit to pass the beautiful gleaming chariot. Roars of laughter and applause could be heard on the hotel grounds. Months later, people would mention the scooter and the ingenuity of the two young men.

In the early mornings, I would walk the dog up a considerable incline and into a small village called Wiswell. Dan would pass me on the way up and start his interval training on the hill. I'd walk Ellie across the fields and then around the village, and Dan would catch up at the top of the hill. Then we'd head for home, ready to start another day's work.

While at work one day, I had a call from the HR Department at the company Dan worked for. The lady that called explained Dan had cut his hand with a Stanley knife and was making his way to the hospital. I was out in the car with Janice, my line manager, so she turned the car around and headed for the local hospital. I found Dan in the waiting room; the cut was deep and ran along the line of his thumb. My worry was that he could have nipped a ligament. A doctor took a look at the cut; thankfully, he didn't seem to think there would be any long-term damage. A nurse stitched Dan's hand up and asked him to attend his nearest medical centre to change the dressing in a couple of days. Janice was waiting outside to take the patient home. Having given Dan lots of sympathy, we dropped him off home and carried on with our day.

All the items from the kit-list that Dan needed gradually came together; from boot polish to swimming shorts, everything was packed and ready for his impending departure.

Dan was travelling to Lympstone on the train the following Tuesday for his three-day pre-joining fitness course, so he picked up his train tickets from Officer Shaw at the recruitment centre. He told Dan that this was his time to shine, and he needed to show the training team what a fearless young man he was. Officer Shaw also explained it would be the most challenging few days of his young life.

Jon and I talked him through the train route, two changes, one at Birmingham New Street and then Exeter St Davids. Not a problem.

Tuesday morning came. He had to arrive in a suit, so I folded a shirt and a tie, placed them at the top of his pile of clothes in his holdall. I gave strict instructions to put his shirt and tie on before reaching Exeter.

The time came to say goodbye. All I kept saying to myself was, "It's only four days." The lump in the back of my throat was making it hard to smile; I didn't want Dan to think it was a big deal because I know he would have felt awful. I tried to say something, but nothing came out. One last hug, and he was gone. The front door shut behind him. I could hear his dad starting the car up; next, Dan's music was blurring away up the road and then nothing.

I gathered myself together and left the house. My head was awash with train times, had he forgotten anything, had he got his phone, etc.

Throughout all of this, Janice was a rock for me. She deserved a medal. Janice had put up with me arriving to work in all states and to see her face that morning gave me so much reassurance that everything would be okay.

So the day just passed by in a blur. Every time I checked my watch, I envisioned where Dan was in the country. He kept in touch via text. The last one came just after Exeter. By this time, I was home. Both Jon and I just sat staring into oblivion, wondering how the hell he would endure the next three days at such a young age.

Dan's name flashed on my phone at about 5.30 pm. I answered straight away; his voice was officious, so I knew he wasn't on his own; he said, "I have arrived, and I'm ok," and that was it. Because he was only 16 and a minor, I now knew that I had to be informed and that we both knew where he was.

As I climbed upstairs that evening, and for the first time, I realised just how much I wanted him to succeed. Or should I say the thought of failure would be so devastating for him after all the hard work he had put in to get this far.

I had a restless night wondering how Dan was getting on. I knew Wednesday was the big day. They were scheduled to be in the gym and put through their paces. If they failed the required gym tests, they would be on the next train home. It was as simple as that.

So, basically, if we didn't hear from him, that was a positive thing. All that day, Janice kept me busy at work, offering the odd word of encouragement here and there. Finally, I headed off home at 3.30 pm. My route took me past Dan's present workplace; I started to wonder what he would do if he failed; I couldn't see him being happy in an engineering role. He would probably do it but never feel fulfilled, and that certainly wasn't what we wanted for him.

Well, no news is good news, or so the saying goes. Jon took me out for a meal to distract me, more than anything. Thursday was the final day, which Dan was not looking forward to at all. This was the day the training team would see what he was made of at Woodbury Common. It arrived and left, still no news.

Jon and I were on tenterhooks all day waiting for a call to let us know if he had passed. Later that evening, Dan texted to say he was in the last twenty out of sixty starters at the beginning of the week. He thought he had done okay but didn't want to jinx it as nothing was official.

It was Friday morning, the sun was shining, and our son was coming home. I went to work, as usual. Both Janice and I were praying for good news. Everybody was texting, trying to find out if he had got through. The call eventually came. Dan's voice seemed so far away, but confidence boomed down the phone. "I did it, Mum, I passed."

All the anxiety and stress of the last few days came out. Tears streamed down my face. It was hard to take in that our son had defied the odds and kept the doubters at bay. Finally, he had passed and was beginning a dream that would soon become a reality.

The rest of the day passed in a haze. Our last day of work for a whole six weeks, and Dan was due home at 8.00 pm that evening. I had a message from Dan saying the train had broken down and he would be arriving at the train station by coach at the usual time.

Jon and I waited outside the train station. We could see the coach turn the corner at the top of the road. We scanned the windows of the coach for a glimpse of Dan. There he was, sat at the back of the coach with the biggest smile I had ever seen on his beautiful face.

By the time Dan had gathered his belongings from the coach, both Jon and I were emotional wrecks. I was trying desperately to hold the tears back and not to cry.

At one point, I noticed Jon looking up at the sky to try and stop the tears from emerging from the corners of his eyes. We didn't want to embarrass him in front of the other two lads who had made the Lympstone journey and had also passed. Both men were in their twenties. One of them made a point of coming over to us and informing us how awesome our son was and how hard he had tried. A colossal wave of pride drifted over us, and for that moment, we were both speechless.

Over the next couple of days, Dan took us over what he had to do while at Lympstone. On Wednesday, the gym work was as predicted. Unfortunately, quite a few of the lads failed and were immediately put on the train home.

In the afternoon, they had to complete a 1.5 mile run in under 10 minutes 30 seconds. With a member of the training team setting the pace. Dan said he set off like a Polaris missile. It was more of a sprint than a run. He said quite a few lads couldn't keep up and faded into the hedgerows. Never to be seen again, and a couple collapsed in the heat as it was warm. He made it but found it challenging, and when he consulted his watch, it was more like nine minutes. Lesson learned. Always be prepared to give more than you think is required.

Thursday was the determination test. It was expected to be the hardest of all tests. Dan said they started by warming up. For part of the test, they had to complete an endurance course that sounded like the one on the final commando test. Dan said it was gruesome. Completing the endurance course took at least several hours. Directly after that, they had to carry each other in a fireman's lift up an unassuming hill along a ridge and back down. Dan was paired with a guy who was probably twice his body weight. Dan's legs buckled on the second charge up the rise, and he dropped to his knees. A member of the training team was there straight away; he said, "If you don't get up and carry on, you are heading home." Dan managed to find the will from somewhere, clenched his teeth and stood up with the muscle man on his back, and staggered up the incline once more. Dan then had to carry the same guy in a cradle lift; it was even more painful than the first lift; you solely rely on your arms for strength. Up and down the incline he went. Daniel said it was the first time he had used the power of positivity. A can-do attitude seeped into his soul, and adrenalin coursed through his veins. He also showed aggression for the first time, which he now uses to accomplish physical things he could not do before. It always pays off to assert positivity in a negative situation. This was his starting point. Now he knows how to overcome the most difficult hurdles.

By the time they had finished, he was literally on his knees. They had crawled through tunnels, stood chest-deep in water, and were told to submerge themselves while holding a rope. They crawled through mud while wet sprinted for one mile, and then repeated the whole process. Then, to everyone's sheer delight, it was over. They had managed to get through the day and could do no more.

The remaining recruits headed back to the grotts to roll their aching muscles and rehydrate. Only seventeen left standing.

Different instances kept cropping up as he reflected on his experience. For example, they were given Marine issue water bottles and told to fill them to the top.

Later, the corporal instructed them to remove their water bottles' lids. He proceeded to walk down the line checking everybody had done what he had asked. A couple of lads had filled the water bottles to the neckline. He stopped and explained that the water missing from the top of their bottles could save their lives one day. To the top, he had said. He then instructed the two lads to pour the water bottle over their heads and the rest of the troop to follow. The training team member ordered them to clean the floor immediately and be ready for inspection in 10 minutes.

The realities of what the corporal was trying to teach them were the realities of war and the dog-eat-dog approach. Dan understood the message the corporal was trying to purvey. Everything they do, they do for a reason.

While the trainees were at Lympstone, they were expected to keep everything clean and tidy in the grots. Everybody pulled their weight, apart from one lad who thought it was beneath him to clean the shower room or mop the floor. However, he would quite happily shout instructions to the other lads from his bed. This really irritated the remaining trainees, especially Dan.

The ironic thing was that he was awarded 'Recruit of the Week', which nobody on the course thought was valid. The punch line obviously came later, when he just managed to scrape through foundation week and then decided it was not for him.

The lads that had made it through the three-day course were each presented with a certificate. This certificate would undoubtedly give the recipient bragging rights, that was for sure.

Dan also came home with the military issue boots the Royal Marines use. Their training team advised them to break the boots in before the start date. They suggested the recruits walk several miles to break them in. Once they felt comfortable, running in short bursts would also work to their advantage.

The training team had also educated them on boot polishing. After every outing, the boots would be treated to a relatively long, laborious polish. The funny thing was he hated polishing his school shoes. Whether it was a rush job on a Monday morning or a Sunday evening, it had been a job I had taken on without a choice.

Now, Dan would sit on the floor for ages polishing his new boots, making sure they were the finest they could be. I was sent to get a specific boot polish, and only the very highest quality yellow dusters would do.

This small act of discipline sent massive signals out to me. I knew Dan was serious about what he was about to undertake, and I also knew he would make sure he gave his all. Dan had been taught to clean his boots that way, and he would continue to clean them that way. No excuses.

When Dan had arrived home, we displayed the certificate in the lounge for all to see. We opened the patio doors at one stage as we wanted to sit outside; a gust of wind had made the certificate fall to the floor; Ellie decided to pick it up and bring it to Daniel outside. There was a big gasp from all three of us at once as she came bounding over. Ellie dropped the certificate in front of Dan, and with a 'does this belong to you?' look, the remnants of his certificate lay before us with teeth marks and the top corner missing.

Jon and I held our breath as we looked at Dan's expression. His face fractured into a smile, and he patted Ellie on the head and made light of the situation. He thanked her for bringing it to him. Ellie's tail wagged profusely. I could see he was upset, but it had been an accident, and he had accepted it for what it was. Maturity at its finest, I thought as I reflected on how he had handled the whole situation.

PREPARING TO LEAVE

The weekend passed quickly. We had lots of visitors congratulating Dan on his success. Dan was at work on Monday morning, so we had several chats about how to approach the apprenticeship placement he had secured. So, we made an appointment with the Human Resource department at the company where Dan had been working, and it was scheduled for the following day. In the meeting, Dan explained that he would no longer be taking up the role of apprentice engineer and the reasons why. The company manager, whilst voicing his concerns about losing a good apprentice engineer, congratulated him on gaining a place and was really pleased for Dan. He said he admired his strength of character and would be an asset to the military with his newfound work ethic.

So the meeting was successful, and they wished Dan well for the future. They also asked him if he would like to work notice for a couple of weeks which he was pleased to do, as the money would come in handy.

The summer flew by. Dan received a date to start his 32 weeks of training and a kit list. There was an iron at the top of the kit list; we thought it could prove challenging. So we bought Dan an iron, and from that day, I have never ironed any clothes for him. I showed him the basics and let him get on with it. He has the battle scars to prove it, and a couple of irons later, he is pretty adept at it. Jon made him a perspex A4 template so he could get to grips with folding his tops correctly.

Next was a sewing kit and how to sew a button onto a shirt! He didn't like it that much, but it needed doing. Finally, from washing lights and darks separately to needlecraft, Dan had mastered basic housekeeping skills.

The next event on Dan's calendar was to pick up his GCSE results from school. The night before, he was apprehensive, probably because it was the only thing standing between him and his dream.

The morning of the results, he carried out the same routine, run, weights, shower. Once he had his protein shake, he was ready to face his results. Jon and I were both anxious and excited at the same time. He had put in the effort, but had it paid off?

We drew up outside Daniel's high school. His friends, including Cameron, had gathered and were waiting for him. They were all prepared to deal with this ordeal together. So off they went into the sports hall to collect the infamous brown envelope.

Dan soon appeared with the envelope clutched to his side. I couldn't read his face from the angle he was approaching. My heart was beating so fast; I felt sick. I wanted this to be over now. He launched his self into the car and handed the envelope to us in the front. Jon opened it, and I scanned the information. He had passed nine out of the ten GCSEs he had taken, all grades 6 or 7, which was absolutely brilliant. All his hard work had paid off. We were so proud of him. He had managed to overcome the many hurdles in his way and made sure those hurdles would not define him as a person in the future. Champagne popped when we arrived home; both Jon and I wanted him to know just how proud we were of him and congratulate him on the journey he was about to take.

Dan was itching to start his new career in Lympstone. With the money he had earned over the summer, he could now buy some new clothes and most items on the kit list, and he could keep £200.00 aside for other things that could only be purchased on the base.

Over the next couple of weeks, he said his goodbyes. The days and then the hours crept down, and suddenly it was the day before. My boy was about to fly the nest at 16 years of age. Every time the doorbell rang, people came to wish him well. I could not contain my tears; they rolled down my face throughout the day. I couldn't eat anything and was dreading the following morning when I had to say goodbye to my son. We checked through the kit list several times, making sure he had everything.

Sometimes Dan would come and sit down on my bed, and we would have many conversations about different subjects. From world famine to the beautiful new baby next door. Tonight was no exception, and with Ellie in close pursuit of Dan, they both sprawled on the bed and snuggled up to me. I felt I needed to reassure him that Jon and I would be just fine without him and that we were 100% behind him. We talked about all sorts as usual. Eventually, looking at the young boy next to me, I could see tiredness washing over him, I shooed him and

Ellie out of the bedroom, and within minutes I could hear Dan cleaning his teeth before heading off to bed. My thoughts were whirling around. I gave myself a pep talk about being strong and not making it difficult for him to say goodbye in the morning. I desperately did not want to cry in the morning.

Dan was up bright and early the following morning. I could hear him singing in the shower to his favourite tunes from his phone. He was happy, and that is all a mother wants for her child. I cooked a hearty breakfast; it would be a long day for him in more ways than one.

That moment came all too soon. Dan was dressed the same way as last time, suit on with T-shirt, shirt and tie in bag. He crossed the lounge and put his arms around me. I held back the tears but could feel my bottom lip trembling. I couldn't find the words I wanted to say. Instead, I looked up to see him looking directly at me. In that split second, he knew just how much I loved him, which was all that was required. He headed to the front door with his bag, one last cuddle from his faithful labrador, Ellie, and, "I love you, Mum." The front door shut, and he was gone, for how long we didn't know.

Janice was waiting in the car park, our usual meeting place. She didn't make a fuss, and she didn't ask anything. She just glanced over and instantly reassured me without saying a word.

Gradually as the day passed by. I started to mention his name without having a massive lump in my throat. In my mind, I kept wondering where he was in the country at that precise moment. I knew he was getting ever closer to his destination and a way of life that would either make him or break him.

We had instilled in Dan from the outset that it was a massive undertaking. He had to be prepared for his worst nightmare. If it was better than that, it was a bonus. Dan had spent several months reading books on motivation. The most inspiring one was David Goggin's 'Can't Hurt Me', a genuinely influential read. I hoped we had given him all the tools required to fulfil his dream.

I arrived home that evening, feeling bereft. I did not know when we would see our son again or what state he would be in when we next met. I was expecting a call from him, but it would only be the obligatory call to let me know he had arrived.

Sure enough, the phone rang. I could hear what seemed like a deep gruff voice replying to my, "Hello." It was Dan trying to be manly. I don't know for whose benefit. He was probably standing next to the corporals.

We managed a quick conversation. The training team had checked all Dan's kit and had confiscated the chocolate I had sneakily put in his bag. He also said that his phone would follow the chocolate and that he would ring when he could. I managed a "Love you," before the line was dead.

Jon was desperately waiting for news. All I could string together was, he had had his chocolate confiscated before the tears started to roll. Before I knew it, I was crying like a baby. Jon was going the extra mile to comfort me, but nothing helped.

After the waves of pain subsided and with swollen eyes, I knew that I needed to get myself together. I had to gather what strength I had left and put the whole situation in perspective. So I ventured upstairs with Ellie by my side, and we settled down on the bed. The next I knew, my upper body was cold, but my feet were nice and cosy. I realised I had drifted off to sleep, and Ellie had positioned herself next to my feet. But, as soon as I awoke, Ellie was there, face next to mine; she looked into my eyes, letting me know she was there. Amid the chaos, she was a great comfort.

The days passed slowly, no news from Dan. Gradually, we fell back into a routine. The nights were drawing in, and it was getting colder by the day. I would take Ellie up to Wiswell each morning, envisaging Dan catching up to us on the bend. I often looked back subconsciously, waiting for him to call out on his way past. Jon and I missed him dreadfully. The house seemed so quiet without him. The washing machine was no longer on continually. There was no rush for any gym gear to be dried. The blender stood still with no smoothies to make. His bedroom lay empty.

Ellie would curl up on his bed for hours, waiting for him to come back, but of course, he didn't. A mention of his name, and she would collect her favourite toy and wait by the front door, wagging her tail. She was always disappointed with the result.

FOUNDATION

Dan rang on Saturday evening. He had been given his phone back for two hours, and he seemed in good spirits. Dan had been placed in a side room with three other lads. The rest of the troop were in one room with beds down each side. They were to be in this block for two weeks; then, they would move into a permanent unit they could call home.

Dan explained that everything they did was at a hundred miles per hour. Even eating was under the clock, shovelling as much food as possible into your mouth in the time allocated. I do understand the reasoning behind this. When you are in a warzone, you are unlikely to see breakfast, lunch, or dinner. You would eat what you could when you could.

Dan mentioned he had very little sleep as he had so much to prepare for the following day. All his clothes had to be hand-washed, dried in the 'drying room', then ironed along with all his bedding each day. I never thought I would ever hear Dan say that there weren't enough hours in the day,

He had all his hair shaved off. Everybody now looked the same. They were now officially called Nods because every time they sat down, they would inevitably nod off.

Military uniforms were issued to all troops from drill to gym. They would have to march everywhere from now on. Dan spent most days in the gym and even more on the parade ground getting to grips with the drill. In marine training terms, they called washing, ironing, and cleaning 'admin'. Orders for the following day were put up in the evening, and the troop had to make sure they had the correct uniform to fulfil those duties. They had to make sure they had all uniforms and equipment ready for the following day.

Dan was issued with boots after passing his PRMC, which he had lovingly broken in. He now had another pair of drill boots, and in his opinion, they were the most unforgiving boots known to man. They were black, and he spent hours polishing them with an old toothbrush to ensure the polish was embedded into the leather. These boots were worn most days at some stage, so they needed to be as good as new and ready for action every day, so polishing them became a nightly chore.

Over the next few weeks, we gleaned lots of information from his intermittent phone calls.

He explained that if any of the troop failed admin, drill, or general duties, the whole troop suffered. Therefore, it was in their interest to work together to achieve their goal. If they failed to do so, they paid the price.

Dan kept himself to himself for a couple of weeks. He was probably trying to get the measure of his new roommates. There were different characters around him, arrogant, cheeky, funny, lazy, quiet, all wanting the same thing—a Green Beret, while also trying to get to grips with this new world he had thrown himself into so willingly. Some conversations with him were short and tense due to all the jobs he still had to do before laying his head on his pillow. In those first few weeks, he rarely slept for more than a few hours at a time.

When he rang, I could sense the weariness in his voice, but never once did he moan about anything. As a young lad stepping out into the big wide world, people assume you naturally fall into the adult bracket, especially training to be a Royal Marine Commando. He was, in fact, a boy.

Dan had to shave every morning even though there wasn't a bristle on his face. He would gently roll the wet razor around his face to give the impression he knew how to shave when the time came.

Dan loved the gym. He initially struggled climbing the thirty-foot high ropes, but there was a knack to it as with most things. He took extra lessons in the evening, and before too long, he was flying up the rope no problem. If the training team saw someone struggling, help was there. The problem with men is that asking for help is a sign of weakness. They would rather fail and get on the next train out of Lympstone than admit they needed help.

Dan wasn't afraid to ask. He picked up a lot of what he would call essential info by watching how the other lads did things, spoke, and acted. Not forgetting he had never been in the company of so many men before. The embarrassment of taking your clothes off in front of other people went out of the window after a couple of days (he often wanders about the house with no clothes on. It is now normal to him).

The tradition of going commando, in the buff, comes from the Royal Marines. So sleeping in a clean bed with nothing on after having had a shower makes sense.

Over the next couple of weeks, the sixty-strong troop started dwindling. Some lads realised it wasn't for them; others left because of medical conditions. It was the nature of the beast. One of the most brutal training regimes, globally, is bound to result in a casualty or two.

In foundation, nobody was allowed any chocolate at all. One of the corporals from the training team spotted a troop member in the NAAFI buying a Mars bar. All of the troop was summoned to the red room a short time later. The offender was brought to the front and asked to empty his pockets, and there it was for all to see, the offending weapon, the Mars bar.

The Nod was instructed to open it and eat it while the rest of the troop were told to bring their water bottles into the room. The corporal ordered the troop to pour the water from their canisters over their heads whilst the offender enjoyed his Mars bar. The recruits then had to get all their A4 folded tops and throw them at the offender.

The corporal instructed the troop to make sure the room was left immaculate. The now wet tops were to be washed, dried, ironed, and folded by 6.00 am the following morning, ready for inspection.

The offender was mortified and felt guilty that the troop would have a sleepless night trying to put things right because he couldn't follow a simple order.

Dan had all his chocolate confiscated on day one. He was invited to the corporal's office for a chat to see how he was settling in. Dan marched in and saluted the corporal who was eating his chocolate. He wanted to burst out laughing but didn't think it appropriate. The corporal even offered him a bar which he reluctantly turned down for fear of a repeat performance of the day before. (Dan now says, looking back, there were so many funny instances like this. It wasn't all doom and gloom).

The troop's last thing before leaving foundation was a night field exercise on Lympstone's bottom field. They had several lectures leading up to this point and were now starting to put what they had been taught into practice.

In this exercise, the harbour was square. The troop had their first taster of the ration packs. Everyone had to do sentry duty. During the night, the heavens had opened, and at one point or another, the lads manning the sentry on all four corners had got soaked through. They were instructed to put their dry uniform on before climbing into their sleeping bags for a two-hour snooze, which sounded logical. They would have to put their wet clothes back on when they awoke, which Dan said was the most awful thing ever. This was called 'wet and dry'. He would have to get on with it as they practised this all the time. They also had to put a dry pair of shoes on before getting into their sleeping bags (for obvious reasons).

Dan said he had enjoyed his first night under the stars but needed to work on his field kit muster. The corporal had pulled him up for his eating irons, not being clean, and for not eating all his rations. Dan was told that he must use all the food for energy for the rest of the day and, in future, eat everything that he was packed, regardless of whether he was hungry or not. Dan understood and hadn't looked at it from that perspective before. Now it made total sense.

Well, Dan had completed Module 1 and had started the transition from civilian life to military life. Although it had been a challenge and a huge learning curve, he appeared to be making significant progress.

Week three started well. Dan was looking forward to weapons training and going to the armoury. The first thing Dan had to master was disassembling and reassembling a gun in a set time. He also had to be assessed on his swimming technique, treading water, and jumping from height into the pool.

Dan had previously experienced the pool on his PRMC and was aware of what they were looking for. This task did not phase him at all. He had practised swimming at the local swimming pool and had perfected his stroke under Jon's instruction.

All the troop were lined up next to the pool. The first task was to swim a length. Dan's line jumped into the water and began to swim. He could hear a commotion behind him but carried on to complete the task.

One of the lads in the troop had forgotten to mention he couldn't swim. So a member of the training team dived into the water to pull him out. Seemingly, he was pretty adept at treading water. Forgive me for thinking it would be imperative for you to know how to swim if you wanted to be a Royal Marine. Needless to say, he was on the train by late afternoon on his way home.

Dan settled into his new accommodation, which would be his home for the foreseeable future. There were six lads in his room, and the troop took over a floor in a block. It was basic, but it served a purpose.

They had been guided through all the basics, from making their bed to ironing their uniform in the first two weeks, now all the knowledge they had gained would be put into practice. Everything had to be immaculate. From shoes polished to creases in shirt arms. If the training team, upon inspection, noticed anything wrong with their kit, everybody in the troop would suffer. One of the notorious things each troop faced if they failed to follow orders was the tank. The whole troop would have to jump into the tank. An ice-cold water tank, great in the summer, not so in the winter.

Dan settled into his room. He spent hours cleaning his kit. They started to work as a team in the room. One lad would clean all the boots, and another would do the ironing. They finished their admin when everyone had finished, and everything was of the expected standard. They spent most of the evenings and well into the early mornings, trying to get things right.

Slowly but surely, they were quickening up and getting used to the repetitive chores.

On the third weekend, they had an inspection at 8.00 am. If it all worked out well, the troop would be allowed some free time to do what they wanted. The troop pulled together and got their wish—eight hours of freedom, from 12.00 pm until 8.00 pm.

Dan caught the train to Exeter with a couple of his roommates. All any of them wanted was food and a pint. Dan was underage and had been told if he was caught inebriated at any time during his training, he would lose his place at Lympstone.

They left the train and headed for the main shopping mall. All the top branded takeaways were on the main esplanade. Following all the tasteless food they had endured on the camp, which undoubtedly served its purpose, they ate a burger and a milkshake, which tasted delicious, beyond expectation. They wandered along aimlessly, trying to find their bearings.

Dan and the boys headed to a local bar to meet the rest of the troop. By this time, some of the lads were onto their third pint, and the jokes and stories had already started. Dan, although on lemonade, enjoyed the camaraderie of being with the troop.

The time passed quickly, and before they knew it, they had to catch the train back to Lympstone. By this time, a few of the lads weren't looking the greatest. Alcohol-induced, obviously. They all managed to get back to the grotts in time for the landing call. The corporal would check that all of the troops were back on site before leaving for the evening.

Just that tiny amount of normality in their lives reinvigorated them for another week. It gave them something to look forward to and to aim for. As all of them knew, if anybody let the troop down this week, they wouldn't be heading anywhere. They were allowed out on Sunday, but Dan decided just to chill and get some rest ready for the week ahead.

Dan chose to finish off his ghillie; they are made from unravelled sandbags, and when retied and shaped, it sits on top of their helmet as a cover. It is supposed to resemble a clump of grass and is essentially used when stalking the enemy. He had almost perfected it. A few stems of grass before slithering into the undergrowth, and nobody would know he was there.

We received an email one evening inviting us to a family day in two weeks. I was ecstatic at the thought of seeing Dan and spending some quality time with him over the long weekend he was due to have. The mood in the household changed to one of excitement. I spoke to Dan about bringing him anything down, clothes, food, etc., to make his life easier. The reply was boot polish and some dusters; how life had changed. A few months ago, it would have been spicy crisps and diet coke.

I wasted no time on booking a cosy cottage about eight miles from Lympstone. The main priority was to make sure it had a washing machine and a dryer.

My next dilemma was what to wear. Jon and I ventured out on a trip and came back with formal, casual clothing; if such a thing exists. Jon would wear chinos, and I, a navy dress.

Everything was now in place, and we managed to speak to Daniel a few times in the week leading up to the family day.

The troop had been practising drills on the parade ground for most of the week. They had also been in the gym perfecting rope climbs. Dan sounded quite happy and was looking forward to having a long weekend away from the base. I had no doubt he would be in his element, showing us around the base before we started our weekend together.

A WEEKEND AWAY

We left on Thursday at lunchtime. It was a six-hour drive down to Lympstone, and we stayed overnight at the cottage to be up bright and early and arrive at the training centre at the required time of 7.45 am.

After we arrived at the cottage, we unpacked and walked to a nearby restaurant for a bite to eat. We were that excited to see our son the following day; I couldn't sleep. I must have drifted off in the early hours to be awoken by the alarm clock, and it was still dark when we left the cottage. We followed the instructions given and parked in the car park opposite the training centre. We used the footbridge to cross the busy road and queued with all the other anxious family members.

We spoke to our guide while waiting to be escorted into the training centre, he asked us about Dan. We explained it was his dream to be here and that he was just sixteen. As they are not fully developed at that age, and the training is so complex, it was unusual for the Corps to take them so young. Due to this, he said they must have seen something special in him that made them commit to his training.

Our names were taken, and we were guided to a conference room; tea and coffee were available, and Dan's training team was on hand to answer any questions.

The biggest question of all was soon asked, "How is Dan doing?" The reply was that he was holding his own but needed to organise himself a little better when he was in the field. They didn't seem to have any other issues with him. They also commented on how hard he was trying—all in all, just what we needed to hear.

Then, we were escorted to the indoor parade ground. We made ourselves comfortable in the seated stand and waited patiently for a glimpse of our son. The drill sergeant's voice boomed out, giving orders to the troop to march into the arena. In they came, all synchronised and looking immaculate in the cold morning sunshine.

I caught sight of Dan in the back row. He looked so grown up yet so small amongst the troop. It was remarkable to see how well they marched together and how far they had come in such a short time.

At one stage, I felt overwhelmed; we had not seen Dan for five weeks, and he had changed so much in that time. He was marching in a troop of potential Royal Marines with a uniform on holding his own at just sixteen. Both of us just stared in awe at this remarkable young man.

The troop marched off in one direction, and we were shown to an auditorium. We recognised Tom's parents; they had also been waiting for the coach to return after the PRMC, and Dan had travelled down with Tom five weeks ago. We had a quick chat before the meeting got underway. It was very informative, and the audience was participating in asking questions about the training. The training centre doctor was on hand to guide us through the rehabilitation process when the recruit was unfortunate enough to get injured.

The doctor advised that it was unrealistic to expect a recruit to do the thirty-two weeks with no injuries. They explained many suffered setbacks with broken bones, torn ligaments, etc., and this would undoubtedly result in the recruit being back-trooped according to the week they injured themselves. They would then leave their current troop and join a new troop.

This in itself would be traumatic for the recruit, as they would have built friendships and trust within their troop. They must leave one group to join another and rebuild those relationships once again.

In addition, they said that things get more complex. They start missing home, and reality starts to kick in. Asking advice from parents is usually their first course of action. They asked us to keep encouraging the recruits and not let them give up and that it would be worthwhile in the end.

We left the auditorium and headed for the gymnasium, where the recruits were about to do a routine that had been rehearsed until perfect. It contained several elements, including rope climbing. Dan had no problems with this any longer. Even Tom's dad commented on the fitness of Dan and how easy he made it look. They executed everything from pull-ups to press-ups with precision. I felt so proud of what they had all achieved in such a short time. Safe in the knowledge that it certainly was not beyond the realms of Dan to achieve his dream. He had survived five weeks in a man's world. Watching him both on the parade ground and in the gym, he had put quite a few of the lads to shame. But that's only a mother's opinion.

We next went on a tour of the rehabilitation unit, an extension of the medical centre. A doctor explained that the unit is vital to the fitness of the recruits and marines alike. Dan will undoubtedly pay the unit a visit at some stage or another, even just for advice.

All I wanted now was a hug from my son. That, I suppose, would have to wait until we were clear of Lympstone. We were guided back to the conference room, where we stayed and waited for Dan to appear. We didn't have to wait long before we saw his cheeky smile coming through the door. He looked so smart in his uniform and blue beret.

I just wanted to fling my arms around him but couldn't. He looked shattered. He had dark rings under his eyes and was as white as a ghost. My heart missed a beat or two at his appearance.

I could see these last five weeks had taken their toll on him. I looked at Jon, and I could see he was thinking the same. Not to worry, I thought to myself, he'll be back on track soon. A weekend of rest and nutritious food will sort him out.

Dan offered to take us for lunch in the canteen; we had just left the conference centre when Dan launched into a march. Jon and I tried to keep up with him. A voice came from nowhere screaming at him to lift his arms, which Dan promptly did. Never mind Dan, it put the fear of God in both myself and Jon. We were scuttling along behind him, thankfully reaching the canteen without any more trouble.

The food was average. We had fish, chips, and peas. I couldn't believe how much food Dan had on his plate and how quickly it disappeared. According to a member of the training team. The average recruit will consume six thousand calories a day to sustain his body's activities.

Our next stop on the whirlwind tour was the accommodation block. This is referred to as the grotts by the recruits. We walked up two flights of stairs to a landing with several rooms running off it. Dan guided us to his room. Six self-contained areas with a single bed surrounded by storage, fundamental but serviceable. He showed us where he kept everything. I couldn't believe how organised everything was. I had been trying for years to get Dan to sort out his bedroom like this, and in just five short weeks, it was precision at its finest.

Both Jon and I enjoyed our day at Lympstone. We had learned a lot from the day. It was so informative. We planned to support our son right through, so we knew what he would experience on his journey. We now knew where Dan was and when he talked about Lympstone on the phone, I would be able to envisage his surroundings. Having had a great day, we could now take Dan away for the weekend. We passed through the main gates and over the footbridge to the car; Dan was already starting to relax.

We headed out of the car park and onto the busy road. The cottage was only a few miles away, so we would be there in no time. After asking about his week and receiving no reply, I noticed he was out for the count, fast asleep. My heart reached out to him. Dan was exhausted. We let him sleep until we got to the cottage. Jon woke him gently, and we all stepped inside the homely open-plan cottage. It had everything we needed, and the host had made us a cake to tuck into later, which I thought was a charming touch. Dan's bag was full of washing. It had a strange smell to it. An old-fashioned musty smell lingered when I opened the first bag.

I loaded the washing machine and switched it on. We decided we would try the local pub for food after a recommendation the night before. We ordered drinks at the bar, turned to see Dan once again fast asleep. We ordered takeaway pizzas, finished our drinks, and made a quick exit with Dan. He didn't even have the energy to eat. Dan dragged himself up to his bedroom, and within minutes, he was in the land of nod.

Dan had slept for a total of fourteen hours when he awoke the following day. He looked so much better and was ravenous.

I cobbled a huge breakfast together, and Dan tucked into it like it was the only meal he had consumed in a long time. I had brought his favourite Moroccan sausage, which is made locally in Whalley. It's a Mum thing.

Jon hung out with Dan for the day, and I tackled all the washing and ironing. It would hopefully make his life a little easier in the coming week. I had just finished repacking his bags when they returned from the tank museum. Jon had wanted to visit for years. Every time we went past the sign on our way to Portsmouth to catch the ferry to France, he would mention it.

Dan had started to relax a little and be more like his old self. He had been tense when we picked him up. Probably due to all the pressure he was under to get things right. Dan had lots of tales to tell us, and as he remembered them, they came tumbling out. A few mornings before, the troop gathered for a five-mile run. The PT had set off at breakneck speed, and the recruits had to keep up. Dan noticed a couple of lads struggling with the pace and slowed up to run next to them and encourage them. When the run was over, the commanding officer pulled him to one side, thanked him for trying to help the weaker recruits, but he advised him to concentrate on himself. The time would come in training to help and encourage one another, but they had not reached that point yet. Dan had estimated the troop would be considerably smaller by the end of the weekend. There had been several moans and groans from his roommates, and he admitted a couple of them were falling by the wayside.

Dan had made a conscious decision to speak with the other lads who were further on in training. Soon he gleaned that life would get more manageable in the coming weeks. He also learned that the detail the training team was encouraging them to show would stick with them until the end of their military careers.

It would eventually become second nature to do the tedious tasks he was trying to overcome now. He knew he just had to hang on in there and give it 100%.

All too soon, Sunday morning arrived, and it was time to drop him off at Lympstone. I gave him an almighty hug then slithered back into the car before Dan could see the tears once more cascading down my face.

As we watched him cross the footbridge and disappear into camp, the feeling of helplessness was overwhelming; I felt sick with the realisation that I couldn't make things better for him as I had done when he was a small boy.

During the drive home, my thoughts were in overdrive. I felt like I was back to square one. I could not cope with my son moving on, and I had to deal with his career choice. I needed to deal with being made redundant; life as I knew it had changed, and I needed to get a grip.

Many positives came out of the weekend. After I had stopped feeling sorry for myself, I rebooted and decided to decorate Dan's bedroom and treat him to a new bed. He had a high sleeper because the room was small and a desk fitted under the bed when he needed to study. We could get rid of all that now and get him a double bed, so it was comfortable for him when he did come home. By throwing ourselves into a project, the week flew by.

Dan had rung on Saturday morning to inform us that he had the day off and was planning to sort his webbing out and would say no more. At last, I heard an inkling of confidence in his voice. I could hear him laughing and joking with the other lads in his room, which incidentally were not the original lads that had started with him. The other five had left through injury or a career change.

Jon and I decided we needed to become more active. We walked quite long distances with Ellie most days, but he thought there was a need for more activity; therefore, we signed up at the local gym, Harris Fitness. Owners Emma and Rob were just what the doctor ordered. They set programs for us to follow and gave us lots of encouragement. Jon enrolled in spin lessons, and I battled on with cardio. This inadvertently stopped the negative thoughts I was having, and positivity returned.

Dan would advise his dad about exercise, and he would reassure me the tyre hanging around my waist would not be there for long.

Dan called us most evenings to give us a quick low down on his day. He was now on module two and was about to embark on a three-and-a-half-day exercise called Marshall Star. The exercise included basic fieldcraft and soldiering skills. Over the last week, they had been to lectures regarding map reading and first aid and tested on weapon handling. So basically, once again, they would practice what had been taught.

Dan enjoyed being outside and was looking forward to trying out his map reading skills.

He had been out with one of his dad's friends who used to be in the Paras. He had taken him over the moors in Yorkshire and had advised him on map reading. So he felt pretty confident.

We wouldn't hear from him until the end of the week. We wished him well and told him to be careful.

The week dragged on until Thursday evening. The phone rang, and it was Dan. He was exasperated. His legs were sore, but he was excited about what he had learned and happy he had proven his worth. To get to the meeting point, they navigated in the dark using three grid reference points. During the day, they had practised stalking. The idea was to get as close to the training team as possible without being noticed. If you got within 150 metres, a shot was fired.

They had set up a harbour in a woodland block. The nights hadn't been too cold, and it was the first time they had eaten their rations hot, followed by a warm chocolate drink.

Once again, upon returning from a field exercise. There is a kit muster where the training team checks your kit to make sure it is clean. Unfortunately, some of the lads, including Dan, were just not getting it right.

Saturday morning came, and one of the training team decided to spend his day showing them how to do a kit muster properly. He brought all his kit over. He instructed the lads to roll around in the mud. The corporal did the same. He cleaned his stuff with them and showed what was expected, from cleaning to packing their Bergens. This corporal from the training team did this in his own time, which I thought was very selfless. By showing the lads step by step the penny dropped, field exercise kit muster was no longer a problem from that day. All through training, Dan's training team have gone the extra mile for recruits in their charge, which is impressive.

One more lad put his chit in after this exercise. This means they would like to leave. You can only chit after the first month has passed. You must report to the commanding officer and state your reasons. Dan says it is sad sometimes because they do not think it through before leaving, so they inevitably reapply later.

Dan and the boys from his section decided to order a takeaway on Saturday night. Until around week eight, this is forbidden. All the boys got involved, and pizzas galore were ordered. While waiting for the delivery, he talked about the exercise he had just done. He said he had just covered sentry duty and was dozing off when all hell broke loose. A tremendous bang, and then the sky lit up like somebody had just flicked a switch. Gunshot could be heard flying through the air; the noise was deafening. He jumped out of his sleeping bag and dived into the dense undergrowth for cover. His automatic reaction was to reach for his rifle and start firing. Dan said it was incredible how everybody had reacted in the same way. He also commented that he wouldn't have known what to do six weeks before, so they were progressing in the right direction.

The following week flew by, and Dan rang on Thursday. They had an inspection of the grotts at 7.30 am, so all hands were to the pump. He also mentioned he was looking forward to PT the following day as it was close combat. In this lesson, they would learn how to defend themselves using different techniques, unarmed.

Unusually, he didn't ring on Friday night, so I texted him to see if all was well. He replied that he was ok. Call it mother's intuition, but I knew something wasn't right.

A BUMP IN THE ROAD

It was Saturday, and Jon was off for the weekend, so we decided to have lunch out and do some Christmas shopping in Skipton, and we visited our favourite restaurant. During the meal, my mobile flashed Dan's name. I answered. He said that he had caught the train to Exeter with the boys. He had enjoyed the armed combat lecture the day before. The lads had carried out some of the different techniques on each other, and this morning he had woken up with a sore neck, headache, and his chest felt heavy.

It sounded like he could have been coming down with a cold. He was in Exeter. I told him to get some cold and flu capsules and try and get some rest. I thought he was on week eight, and it was beginning to take its toll. He rang on Sunday saying the lads had been out on Saturday night, and he hadn't felt up to it. He had chilled out and watched a movie on his tablet.

I had eventually fallen asleep late into the night worrying about Dan. It was unusual for him to complain of being unwell. Even as a child, he had very rarely been ill and had an exemplary record for attendance at school. I rang him on Sunday, at lunchtime, to see if the relaxation and a restful night's sleep had helped. Dan said he felt much the same, like someone was sitting on his chest. He reassured me he would seek medical advice if he didn't feel any better the following morning.

Having had a fitful night's sleep and feeling bleary-eyed, I glanced at my phone to see if Dan had texted. I could hear Ellie stirring downstairs. Her tale hit the radiator several times, and she let out a rather loud yawn. I glanced at the clock. It was 5.30 am. I dragged myself out of bed, put my scruffy dog walking clothes on, and made my way downstairs. By this time, Ellie was in full song, and fed and watered; we made our way up to Wiswell. The hour's walk in the cold morning air did me a world of good, and as usual, my thoughts centred around Dan and hoping he was feeling better. I felt refreshed and ready for the day ahead; shower, breakfast, then work. I met Janice in the usual car park. We discussed the day's business then headed off to catch up on some administration.

It was later than usual when I pulled on to the drive having had the day from hell at work. It was Monday, the most challenging day of the week. As I was gathering my bags together, I noticed Dan had texted me. It read, 'Ring me as soon as possible, don't worry'.

I walked into the house to be greeted by Jon, confirming my worst fears. Dan was on his way to the hospital in Exeter. I rang his mobile, no reply. I decided to ring the medical centre at Lympstone. They confirmed he was on his way to the hospital, and a doctor would ring us shortly.

Meanwhile, I continued to try Dan's mobile, and eventually, he answered. Dan explained he had completed a drill that morning then a run. On the run, he said he had struggled. The training team encouraged him to keep moving forward, which he did for fear of being back trooped.

He managed the run, but only just, and attended a lecture on map reading after lunch. His commanding officer asked to see him. He wanted to know why there had been such a dramatic change in how he had performed that morning on the run; he was usually up near the front, and usually, a run so short wouldn't have been a problem for him.

Dan explained how he felt, which was difficult because he had lots of aches and pains continually due to the intensity of the training regime. But this was different. It had utterly zapped his energy, and his neck and chest were so painful.

His Commanding Officer sent him to the medical bay, where they checked him over. He was running a temperature, and his neck was stiff. He was being sent to the hospital, as the doctor suspected he might have meningitis.

Dan was assessed and put on antibiotics, and quarantined. Anybody that came in or out wore a mask. He was put on a drip and told to rest. Dan had never been in hospital. He had just turned sixteen, and he was three hundred miles away from his parents.

A corporal from the training team stayed with him until he was in bed and then left. Dan was in a lot of pain. I tried to make him feel a little better. He just kept repeating how ill he felt. We wanted to reassure him that he was in the right place and to get some rest. I said I would ring in the morning.

After a sleepless night, I rang the Royal Devon and Exeter Hospital to find out if he was any better and what was the next step. He was my son and only sixteen, but they would not discuss anything with me but could pass on a message to Dan. I was amazed that they had refused to speak to me over the phone.

Within minutes the phone rang, and it was Dan. He still felt awful and didn't know what was going on. We spoke to the doctor at Lympstone, and he confirmed they were running tests; he also told us they would be giving Dan a lumbar puncture as they were testing him for cranial meningitis, among other things. We were in two minds about whether we should head down to Exeter or not because he would not be able to see us as he was in quarantine. We decided to hang fire and wait for his results.

Later that morning, the Padre from Lympstone visited Dan on the ward. Masked up and with a handful of goodies for Dan, he entered the room. He instantly made Dan feel at ease; more importantly, he brought some conversation. They talked about Dan's aspirations for the future and the Corps. He left with a promise of a return visit the following day and asked if he needed anything, which was so kind. I felt so grateful someone had taken the time to make sure he was okay.

We knew we would have to travel down to collect him, so we started organising time off from our employers that day. Janice told me not to worry and to take as much time as was needed.

Dan had asked his dad about the lumbar puncture and whether it would hurt. Jon told him straight that yes, it would, but it needed to be done.

The doctors came later that afternoon to complete the procedure; Dan said his body raised itself from the bed by two feet when they inserted the needle into his spinal cord.

They tested him for various illnesses, and everything came back negative, including the lumbar puncture, which was good news.

According to the doctor at the hospital, his illness was a virus. He explained that because they put their bodies through such rigorous exercise, their immune system can become weak, and a virus that would usually be shrugged off takes hold.

Dan spent another night in hospital, ate well, and slept well but still didn't feel well. When we next spoke, I could feel him getting anxious about his return to Lympstone. One thing Dan already knew was that he would have to leave his present troop. We tried to allay his fears, but he didn't want to talk about it until he heard it from the horse's mouth.

Dan returned to Lympstone the following day. He spoke to the doctor, and it was agreed he would take two weeks off. He would then be assessed for health and fitness and decide whether re-hab would be necessary upon his return.

We had to make the long journey to pick him up. The doctor said he would not be able to travel on public transport due to the strength of the pills he was taking.

We travelled down on Friday, stopping overnight in Exmouth in a lovely hotel that looked across the bay. The hotel itself was busy with Christmas parties, but that didn't stop us from enjoying the unplanned mini-break. It was nice to wake up to the sound of the sea hitting the harbour wall on a cold winter's morning. We left the idyllic setting with a vow to return in the summer.

Dan rang to say he had been authorised to leave. We met him in the car park and what an angry young man he was. There wasn't much point in talking to him because he was deaf to anything we were trying to say. So, it was a long journey home in more ways than one.

We arrived home in good time, beating a lot of the weekend traffic. Jon and I left him with his thoughts that night and his Xbox. I could hear him chatting to his long-time friend Cameron. If anyone could change his mood, it was Cam.

The following day Dan felt less tense. Remembering what the training team had told us about injuries on our open day to Lympstone. We decided to broach the subject.

At first, we hit a brick wall. Then Dan realised we knew more about the subject than he did. The thoughts Dan was having were utterly different from reality. He thought he had let us down, and the Corps would think badly of him because there seemed no actual cause for his illness. Therefore, was he swinging the lead?

We talked everything over, and he seemed a lot calmer. Gradually over the next week, with healthy food and plenty of rest, Dan was getting back to normal. His chest still felt heavy, and he was tired, but mentally, he was in a positive place.

Dan travelled back to Lympstone on the train for the last week before Christmas. The idea being he would get the all-clear from the medical team and move all his gear over to the new troop he would be joining in January.

Everything ran according to plan, and the following week Dan arrived home for Christmas.

He started to relax as soon as he arrived home. He had decided to stop by and see Rob at the gym to see if he could train there while he was home. 'No problem,' was the reply from Rob. Dan decided to focus on his running as he had just started carrying weight while running at Lympstone. So the treadmill got a battering each morning.

I could hear him coughing during the night, and he seemed to be unable to breathe deeply without his chest hurting. I was convinced he had a chest infection. So with that knowledge, I asked Janice, my manager and good friend, for any advice on a quick fix. She suggested we roll Dan on his front and play the drums on his back to loosen the catarrh. In addition, she advised him to rub Vicks on his chest each evening as it would help him breathe a little better during the night.

We had lots of fun over Christmas. He spent quality time with his brothers. They took him bouldering, and Dan seemed to feel a lot better, so he convinced us he was on the mend.

Jon and I entered the annual 10K local race between Christmas and New Year. Over the last couple of weeks, I had been nursing an injury in the knee area, and it didn't seem to be getting any better. I didn't want to aggravate the knee further, so Dan suggested running in my place. He said it would be a helpful exercise for him to do.

On the morning of the race, I had organised to meet a dear friend of mine, Joanne. Her husband, Adam, was also running in the race. Therefore, it made sense to leave our car and belongings at their house. We could then walk down to the start of the race together. Dan's mate, Cameron, was also running, so he met up with him.

Soon the race was well underway. It was a popular race with runners competing from across the county. Joanne and I chatted about life in general. She had recently lost her mother to breast cancer after a hard-fought battle, so it had been a heartbreaking time for her. This would be the family's first Christmas without their beloved mother. Her Mum had been the backbone of the family. She was her everything and to no longer have her by her side, she felt utterly lost. Her husband had been an enormous strength to her, as was her family. Although she was hugely charismatic, the huge personality that lit up every room she entered had dulled, and she was in immense pain.

Joanne had a real soft spot for Dan and would text him when he was away, giving him some advice to help him on his journey. As a boy, she encouraged him to grow into an intelligent young man. Additionally, she was always there for me. The odd text would lift my spirits. We would meet up and put the world to rights over a bottle of wine. Basically, we leaned on each other for support and managed to steer one another through the darkest of days.

The race winner came past the finish line to a huge roar, followed gradually by other contestants. Dan was the first to go through from our group, excluding Cameron, who had well and truly nailed it in well under an hour. Dan used to say he was like Forest Gump. He could run for miles without feeling tired, and not a drop of sweat would be seen. Jon and Adam were next to pass the finish post. On the walk back to Joannes, Dan complained his chest was tight. However, he wasn't overly concerned as this was the first time he had exerted himself for a while. He had enjoyed the experience. Now for bacon butties and a nice warm brew.

Dan spent New Year's Eve with Cameron and his family. He came home on New Year's Day 2020 looking worse for wear and vowing he would never drink again.

The following day Dan left with his dad to catch the train back to Lympstone. He left early, so he could get himself organised for an early start on Monday. He was about to repeat week eight and knew he had a run in the morning and a lecture in the afternoon.

We had spoken at length about how sometimes life throws you the odd curveball, and by dealing with it, it strengthens who we are as a person. Dan seemed to take on board what we had said and seemed a lot happier than he had been previously.

Having finished work for the day on Monday, I made my way home. The roads were unusually busy, considering we were still in lockdown. The thought of Ellie greeting me at the door with one of the many toys she had received at Christmas brought a smile to my face. The house was now empty once more. I was determined to go to the gym that evening. I had promised Dan I would keep my New Year's resolution. The weather had turned cold as the sun was hidden behind many clouds in the late afternoon.

My phone was buzzing on the seat beside me, and Dan's name was flashing up. My first thought was he had finished early that day and had found time for a chat. How wrong was I?

I answered, quite excited to hear his voice but wasn't prepared for what he said.

The inspection had not gone well that morning, and some of the recruits had let the side down. So as always, there is a price to pay.

They were instructed to get their gym gear on and undergo the sandbanks out in the estuary at Lympstone. This is one of the most strenuous exercises they do. All of them ran into the wet sand as a troop. Trying to maintain their balance, the recruits struggled while their legs sank into the sand. Trying to lift them was so tricky. They had to crawl in the gloopy sand, carry each other an insurmountable distance on each other's backs. They teamed up and ran with telegraph poles on their shoulders while knee-deep in wet sand.

Two hours of torture. They then had to run back to base. Dan was running with the pack. His chest was tight, and he was struggling to get enough air in his lungs. Dan can't remember anything else. He had completely blacked out. Dan was once more taken to the hospital. He was still complaining that his chest hurt, so the doctor sent him for an x-ray.

The results were pretty astonishing. Dan explained that he has two cracks in his ribcage next to his sternum.

The doctor explains that they are old injuries. According to him, they are about six weeks old. He had been experiencing constant pain because his cracked ribs were infected. The doctor said Dan must have been in excruciating pain when he performed any exercise. He also said it was his body's way of telling him enough was enough, and it just shut down, hence the blackout.

Dan also explained he could remember what the likely culprit was. He had launched himself into the undergrowth with his rifle on Marshall Star; he had hit a rock with his chest on the way down, and with everything he was dealing with, he just carried on. The pain worsened as it got infected.

Looking on the bright side, we now knew what had been causing him so much pain, and it was mendable. I had to giggle to myself at the thought of Dan lying on the floor in the lounge. He was being pounded on his back, trying to loosen the catarrh from his chest. It was two cracked ribs that were infected. It must have been so painful.

He was now in the medical centre at Lympstone until they could get the infection under control. Two corporals from his present troop heard the news and paid him a visit in the med bay. They applauded him for his efforts on the mud run with two cracked ribs and told him not to give up as he would make it. He had what it took to be a Royal Marine, and the fact he had not given up until he blacked out showed a scarce quality. They shook his hand then left. Dan was over the moon with their comments, and it made a lasting impression on him.

While Dan was in the med bay, his friend from his original troop, Tom, came in suffering from torn ligaments that would take far longer to heal. From what I can gather, the recruits feel it is a sign of weakness to report to Med Bay. If you are sporting an injury, it will only worsen without treatment and can take a lot longer to heal. However, you will undoubtedly get the odd recruit who should have a ward named after him for no apparent reason.

He seemed to have taken another back troop quite well. I think he was relieved it wasn't something more sinister, and his dream was still doable.

Dan said he wanted to stop at Lympstone and do rehab in Hunter Company. He was in a four-person room. Two of the lads Dan knew from PRMC. He would go to the gym in the medical centre every day and mainly concentrate on cardio. Dan used a spinning bike to exercise. He noticed the lad sitting next to him was eagerly watching Dans' speedometer. Before he knew it, his legs were pumping like clappers, and they were racing against the clock. There wasn't much in it, but Dan conceded, and they shook hands. The guy next to him had been a Royal Marine, so what do you expect? Anyway, that was Dan's excuse.

Over the next couple of weeks, Dan's fitness got back to full strength. Dan and a few more able lads from Hunter Company did a one-night field exercise to ensure they were on the right track to rejoin a troop. One of the training team members carried his Bergan because it would put too much strain on his chest, weighing in at an average of 65kg. He carried his webbing and daysack, which were still quite heavy. During the exercise, Dan did sentry duty for four hours. He said it was a clear night with a full moon. He could recognise some of the constellations in the night sky and wondered if we could see the Plough in our night sky too.

Dan had to be back at Lympstone early the following day. He had an appointment with physio to see whether he could rejoin the training program. He had to do a field kit muster before returning to Lympstone. During this time, the training team inspect all the equipment the recruits have used and cleaned on the field trip. It had been one of Dan's weak points. He passed, so there was no longer anything to worry about on that score. Dan spent the next two weeks making sure he would be fit enough for his gym pass-out in week nine.

At last, he got the all-clear to join his next troop, and low and behold; he is on week nine. He escaped the dreaded week eight, which he was ecstatic about.

Dan also knows he must pass his gym pass-out on the Friday of week nine, or he will be back-trooped once more. He seemed to have everything under control and was looking forward to Friday. They had a gym pass out that covered everything they did in the gym. The training team must ensure the lads are fit enough to move onto the bottom field, an endurance course like no other. In our conversation on Thursday night, we wished him well for the following morning.

When the dreaded call came, we took a deep breath. Dan confirmed that he passed with flying colours. Unfortunately, a couple of lads hadn't made it up the ropes, so they would be given another opportunity before being back trooped for more training. He also says they could have the weekend off if they passed the kit inspection the next morning. It was also suggested they leave the camp overnight. Most of the lads in Dan's troop lived a couple of hours away from the base and headed home. Some of the lads were booked hotel rooms in Exeter for the night, which seemed the only thing for Dan to do. He asked my advice, and we booked him a room in a hotel some other lads were staying in. The big night out was planned. But first, they were booked into the hotel's spa for a massage and then a swim. They were planning to trip the light fantastic in Exeter. I admit I was conscious that he was so young, and he may not be able to get into half the places the lads intended to visit.

I didn't hear from him for the rest of the day and had a sleepless night worrying about him and wondering if he would be okay.

I had taken Ellie out over the fields, and when I came back, I noticed I had a missed call from him. I rang back immediately, and he was tucking into his full English breakfast, having eaten half the buffet before his meal arrived.

Dan explained they had been to the spa then had been swimming in the hotel pool. He had returned to his room to change, fell asleep, and woke up an hour ago starving. So my sleepless night had been in vain; Dan had been tucked up in bed after all. He waited for the other lads to surface, then headed out for some lunch before returning by train to Lympstone.

He was in a far better state than some of the lads. All in all, it probably did them all a world of good. They had a big week coming up, so the release of tension would be just what the doctor ordered. The troop had all formed alliances through their sections and enjoyed each other's company. While cleaning boots and ironing their uniforms that afternoon, all the exploits of the night before slowly trickled out.

Dan seemed to have settled down in this troop. The training team is decent, and the sergeant is fair. The sergeant is from the Netherlands; Dan says he is intrigued by the fact he is only sixteen. In his country and the rest of the world, you have to be eighteen to join the military, especially the elite forces. The reason being is that the body is not fully formed at that age; hence the likelihood of serious injury is high. Maturity comes into it as well; no sulking allowed. One of the training team also joined at sixteen, so they knew what Dan was dealing with. Dan explains the sergeant often uses his age as a lever to encourage the other troops to do better, which he finds hilarious. The old adage, 'If a sixteen-year-old can do it, why can't you?'

One evening I was skimming through my emails when I noticed a joining confirmation code. It was for what I can only describe as a purely male website with ladies in rather compromising positions. I must admit it took the wind out of my sails momentarily. I glanced over in Jon's direction. I had noticed he was spending a lot more time on his phone recently and had a twinkle in his eye.

I asked Jon if he had taken up any new hobbies recently. He looked at me, confused. I then let him have it with both barrels. I told him how disgusted I was. Jon denied all knowledge of it, and I flounced out of the room feeling betrayed.

In the morning, I deployed the silent treatment. Jon kept telling me he had no idea what I was talking about, proclaiming innocence at every turn.

After much debate, Jon took me out for lunch, trying to quash the argument. While paying for the bill at reception, I noticed a message flash up on Jon's phone. It was from Dan. It read, 'Sorry, dad, will sort it with Mum.' The penny dropped straight away. It had been Dan, not Jon. I didn't know what was more terrifying, my son or my partner.

I spoke to Jon and apologised, then rang Dan and told him that I had caught his dad looking at a suggestive 'lady site'. He burst out laughing and suggested I penalise him further. Then after much giggling, he admitted he was guilty. The lads in his room had persuaded him to join, and his poor dad had taken the flak and tried to cover for him. I suggested he should get his own email address from now on, and that was the end of the subject.

Monday morning arrived; week 10, and they left for a five-day exercise on Dartmoor. Dan was a mixture of excited and up for the challenge but also dreading it. I suppose that comes from the anticipation of the unknown. Over the last week, they concentrated on navigational skills and map reading. They had several lectures on the subject and had to complete tests in both areas and another in first aid. With Dan having just left school, he soaked this information up like a sponge. He passed all the tests that came his way. He was now ready for Hunters Moon.

Dan had a recent meeting with his training team. They had encouraged him to take the lead in the section. This was because he had the skills and knowledge to lead this particular exercise because he was the quiet one in the group, and they wanted to see him assert himself.

The conversation came up one night when he rang; he said the lads were older than him by five, six years and thought it would be disrespectful to be instructing them to do things. I explained that age didn't come into it. It didn't matter how old they were; he had the same knowledge as them and was expected to approach it the same way they would. Older or not, he understood what I was trying to say, and hopefully, he went away to think about what I had said, then act upon it. It must be hard for him to raise his head above the parapet, but as his confidence grows, so will his ability to lead.

ALL PART OF THE FUN

A couple of Merlin helicopters landed on the base and took them to their destination. We had to wait five days to find out how everything went. So basically, no news is good news. Anything can happen during an exercise, from injury to exhaustion.

My first night's sleep was uninterrupted. The next few nights, I tossed and turned; I woke up feeling like I had been through a hurricane. Still one day less to worry, and that's how my week played out.

The weather here was cold, with intermittent snow throughout the night. All I could think about was Dan out in this weather, and being on Dartmoor, it would be far more severe.

I switched the television on to hear Storm Kiera was about to hit the south of England. With high winds and torrential rain. The commanding officer had warned them all; they would have to deal with adverse weather conditions, so it wouldn't be pretty. It would be the first time carrying their bergens any distance, so anything could happen.

Friday morning eventually came. I had not had a phone call. Fingers crossed he had made it.

Dan rang that very evening. I could feel his joy down the phone. He'd had such bad luck over the last couple of months, and now things were starting to swing his way. Hunters Moon put to bed.

Amongst so many difficult things he had to do was solo navigating in the dark, with driving snow, for six miles, across one of the remotest parts of Dartmoor was at the top of the list. He admitted that, at one stage, he had never been so frightened in his life. He said he couldn't see two feet in front of him; he was constantly tripping over, scrabbling round in the dark. At one point, he thought he was lost, but he pulled himself together and got back on track. He had made it to the checkpoint in good time, much to his relief. Dan had also had to show survival skills. He had to kill a chicken with his bare hands. He professed to have eaten a chicken's eye and tasted its heart.

The troops had walked for miles, and his feet were covered in blisters, even between his toes; there was no nail left on one of his little toes.

During the many long hours yomping over the countryside, the sergeant would keep morale up by telling the lads of his times in certain warzones. He would also talk about the landscape and its surroundings. He walked with Dan over some rough terrain and spotted a horseshoe sticking out of the ground. The sergeant bent down, plucked it out of the ground and gave it to Dan; with a nod, he said, 'you may need this,' and put it in his bergen. All Dan could think about at the time was 'more weight, not what I need right now'. When he thought about it later, he had been touched by the gift.

Friday morning came. It was a cold crisp morning, and the sun was just beginning to rise. They were told they would have to walk for a couple of hours with their bergens to reach where the coach had parked to take them back to camp.

They seemed to be yomping forever. Yomp up the hill and run down the other side. They had been doing this for nearly four hours. They eventually reached the point where the coach was picking them up. Dan said the boys had just begun to relax; a few smiles manifested through the pain the recruits were feeling, having completed the exercise.

The commanding officer delighted in telling them they had at least another four hours of walking to do. There were many moans and groans, but they all gathered themselves together and once more and started out again. Two miles in, Dan said he was too exhausted to care at this stage. He said he could feel himself staggering all over the road. Every bone in his body hurt, and his feet were on fire. After what seemed like an eternity, they eventually saw the white coach in the distance. Dan said you could feel everyone's pain dissolve and the looks of hope descending onto the recruits' faces, and all eyes were pinned on the coach in the distance.

Dan and the troop understood why they had filled the recruits with expectation, only to pull the rug from under them. Always expect the unexpected and always be ready to give more than you think you have to give.

As I pointed out to him, he had probably got off lightly. Some lads didn't make it, and they would have to do it all over again in the next troop. One lad had misstepped and landed awkwardly, resulting in a broken leg; another had hypothermia. The troop numbers were dwindling as the training team had predicted. Dan had to eat his rations cold due to time, and I believe a lot of spooning was carried out to keep warm in the sub-zero temperatures. He said it was the worst experience he had ever had. But I think in a few months, there will be another one to beat it.

There was a landing call while he was on the phone, so the conversation was cut short. Dan eventually called back and explained that they might not get leave tomorrow due to a couple of lads from their troop going to the galley with dirty hands. They were given a lecture on hygiene and told there would be an inspection at 7.00 am. Dan had hoped for an early night as they had not had a decent night's sleep all week. Due to the morning inspection, this would decrease to a couple of hours at most. Everything would have to be immaculate. They were all hoping for leave on Saturday. The recruits set to and made every effort possible to be granted leave the next day.

Upon arriving the following morning, the corporal inspected each room and found them to be in order. He gave them orders to be back at camp by midnight. Cinderella time, as he called it.

The boys were made up. They caught the train from the base to Exeter, and before long, they were sinking their teeth into a well-earned chicken burger. Dan needed a haircut, so he headed off to the barbers, and then they all met up at the pub. Dan never feels quite comfortable in the pub as he is underage and has had countless lectures on drinking from the training team. He does like the banter between the lads, though.

Before they know it, it's 10.00 pm. The lads are interested in heading to a club for the last hour, so they descend upon one particular club in Exeter. Dan is well aware of the time and is also aware he may not get into the club and might be heading back by himself. They are all queued up outside the club. The bouncer asked Dan if he was with the lads in front; he nodded his head, and they all went through the front doors. This was Dan's first time in a club; he said the atmosphere was electric, and the tunes were banging (I believe this means 'great'). He kept his eye on the time, a few of the lads were very drunk, and Dan decided it was the time to take charge. A few of them made it outside and onto the minibus, he had ordered, then he went back inside to find the rest. Some of the lads were chatting up the opposite sex; others were vomiting in the gents. Dan gathered up the stragglers, and soon all twelve original recruits were on the minibus and heading back to camp.

They arrived in the grotts with five minutes to spare. A few of the lads hung onto the handrail to steady themselves. The corporal calls their names, all present and correct. He started to leave and glanced knowingly at Dan, who was stone-cold sober and had to manage a bunch of intoxicated men all by himself.

The following day Dan had a restful sleep and slept until midday. He had some admin to do later, but that could wait. It would be the first time Dan had been able to have some time for himself since arriving. He decided to have a long soak and try and get rid of the pain he felt in his lower back. The bergen had rubbed Dan's back as he walked. He would have to remember to put tape across his back next time and ensure his top was tucked in. Lesson learned.

Dan rang to let us know they were embarking on a field trip the following week to the Netherlands. They would leave on Thursday to catch the ferry from Dover to Dunkirk, then onto Arnhem to see the war graves of the Battle of Arnhem, which is depicted in the film 'A Bridge Too Far'. The troops were all on a high, a relaxing couple of days. Dan said when the coach was mentioned, the troops couldn't do anything but smile as it meant they could grab a few hours' sleep, whatever the circumstance.

The next time he called, he was on the coach; on the coach, the training team played the movie to see what happened during the battle. Having crossed the channel, the coach made its way up to Arnhem. The recruits arrived early evening. They settled into the accommodation, had some food, and an early night.

The following day after breakfast, they visit the war graves. They are given a tour and an accurate account of the events of the battle. Dan said it tugged at his heartstrings, reading the gravestones and seeing boys of his age and younger giving their lives for the freedom we now have today. The training team laid a wreath, and the recruits wrote messages of condolence to the fallen.

Then, they headed back to the hostel for an evening meal; after dinner, the training team allowed the recruits some free time to explore Arnhem and its nightlife.

They arrived back in the early hours. In fact, Dan said the sun was rising when he crawled into bed for a couple of hours' sleep before leaving.

He said there were some really sad sights at breakfast. He was just tired as he had not had a drink. He had been pre-warned once more by the training team that he was underage.

Having said that, he'd still had a brilliant night with lots of laughs and amusing stories about specific individuals and their drunken antics. The time had come to leave, so the coach made its way back to the port. All that could be heard from the recruits was muffled snoring.

They arrived back at Lympstone late on Sunday night. The training team finished the trip by saying there would be a kit inspection at 8.00 am, leading to a massive groan from the recruits.

Still fresh in his mind after his ordeal on Hunters Moon, the question had to be asked, 'was it still what he wanted to do?' Without a second thought, the reply was, 'Yes, more than ever, Mum.' Good, then we keep going.

That afternoon I had watched Lowry and Son, and thank god I am not like that; we are all protective of our children; I would love to have my son by my side and not go through all the pain and anguish that comes with letting them fly. We brought him into this world to be the best he possibly can be and to reach for the sky and achieve his dreams. If Lowry's mother had supported him and let him fly high, she would have been so proud of him, and he would have had the life she thought he deserved.

Daniel had a huge week coming up. They moved to live fire and had the opportunity to throw high explosive grenades, with expressions of joy, louder than the explosion itself. It is clear that although the training is harsh, the recruit's experience far outweighs the discipline asserted. First, they must master helicopter dunker drills, which I could not do. This simulates a helicopter crash into the water in a variety of scenarios. If you ever wanted to bottle anxiety, the moment before the cab falls into the water in complete darkness, knowing you are about to turn upside down is probably the best time to do it.

The following week, Baptist's walk and run were held. The walk is the practice for the run, which tests the accumulation of everything they have learnt, and the ultimate test to see if they make the grade. It marks the end of phase one pass out in regular military training. The recruits would pass out of training following a test. In contrast, Royal Marine recruits continue training for another seventeen weeks to complete their commando training.

Such a big week. I could tell Dan was nervous. If he passed the Baptist run, we would know for sure that he has what it takes. Tuesday morning arrived, and we would not hear anything until the evening, so it was likely to be a long day.

I met Janice at the usual spot. We chatted briefly about the day ahead, and for a while, Dan was pushed to the back of my mind, but he kept coming back to the forefront. I had that same feeling I had when he travelled down to Lympstone to do his training. The fear of Dan failing today was unbearable. He was settled; he loved being in this troop. If he had to move again, it would be awful. How would I pick him up from that? Around and around it went. Janice reassured me he had got this, and all would be well, and every time my phone rang, we both looked at each other, hoping it wasn't Dan.

If he was ringing at this time, it meant he would have failed. By the time I had finished work and arrived home, I was definitely feeling more optimistic.

The call came about seven o'clock. Dan explained they had called them in one by one. Before it was Dan's turn, two lads from his room were told they had failed, so his heart was in his throat. All the training team members were seated when he walked into the office. He saluted, then was asked to sit down. He admitted he had never wanted something so much as in that moment.

The sergeant began the conversation by congratulating Dan on his attitude, strength, and perseverance. The unwavering smile he had on his face each day was a breath of fresh air. He also commented that he had the ability to become a Royal Marine Commando and would undoubtedly make it. He had passed phase one. 'Better than winning the lottery, Mum,' Dan said. I thought so too.

The rest of the week flew by. We were getting media reports that a virus was sweeping across the globe from China. It sounded a bit far-fetched in the beginning and, like most things, seemed so far away. Nobody really knew how serious it would turn out to be.

Dan had spoken about it before he travelled to Straight Point to complete his rifle training. It was pretty laid back; they had to learn how to shoot from three different distances in and three different positions. Once more, there was a test at the end of the two weeks. Seemingly Dan had a keen eye for it. His commanding officer had asked him where he had learned to shoot. Dan said he had never done it before, and it was probably beginner's luck. The officer told him that it wasn't luck; he was a natural.

Straight Point was an excellent place for the recruits to spend some time. In the early mornings, they would exercise on the beach. As usual, it would turn into a competition; they would do firemen's lifts and run like the wind along the beach, pushing and cajoling their opponents. One afternoon the troop ended up in the sea with the training team and even persuaded the commanding officer to join them. They are human, after all.

I think Dan learned a valuable lesson from all the camaraderie between the training team and the recruits. The sergeant from the Netherlands taught the troops about respect, not just for each other but respect for their surroundings. Dan said he had a very calming demeanour, and in his company, you felt confident and able to complete a task with ease.

He still mentions him now, saying he made a lasting impression on him and hoped he would influence the younger generation in the way he did with him.

Dan's age would be used once more by the sergeant to produce a winning formula. He would make the usual comment, 'How come a sixteen-year-old can do it, and you can't?' It became a standing joke when Dan's name was mentioned. All the lads took it well, and everyone tried that little bit harder.

Obviously, they had work and tests to do while at Straight Point, but it was an altogether different atmosphere. The training team staff would recall situations they had been in, whether it was a theatre of war or when they were training. I think the recruits appreciated their honesty. I know Dan did. The food was shipped in at mealtimes, and it was plentiful. On one of the last nights there, they put a colossal pizza order in, and one of the training team collected it for them.

They returned to camp, and everyone was feeling upbeat; they had heard smatterings of what was happening in the news but probably didn't realise how serious it had become. Their orders were to leave camp and return home as soon as possible. By the last week of March, Dan was on his way home before we entered complete lockdown. They had already sent most of the camp on leave except the recruits due to pass out in the next week or so.

Dan had arrived at week 15, so more or less halfway there. He was devastated that his training was now on hold but happy to be coming home. We had not seen him since Christmas, and he was actually due home at Easter, which was only a couple of weeks away. Some of Dan's fellow recruits had to book flights home to South Africa and St Vincents in the Caribbean, so logistically, it must have been a nightmare.

Jon drove to pick Daniel up from the train station. He said it was bizarre; there were no cars on the road. The usual shops along the way were all closed, and nobody in the park they passed when setting off home. Everybody was behind closed doors, wondering and worrying about what was coming next.

Dan arrived home with bags of dirty washing, the usual smirk on his face, and lots of tales to tell. Both Jon and I were essential workers, so we didn't feel the impact others had to bear. Dan took advantage of the long lie-ins, and he and his friends played Xbox. He kept in touch with his troop through a group chat and enjoyed running every day. He soon digressed into his previous exercise regime and even took Jon under his wing as a gym partner.

We decided to redesign our back garden and turn it into a social haven, as did many others. Before too long, wagons were dropping off the stone, gravel, railway sleepers, and such like to transform our garden.

Before leaving for work one morning, I had asked Dan if he could move the five-ton of hardcore which had just been delivered to the back and into the vast hole that had appeared in Jons design.

Dan was moving the hardcore when I returned after lunch via a wheelbarrow round to the back garden. He was sweating and had taken his top off. The next-door neighbour, Paul, was chuckling to himself; Dan was oblivious to three girls continually wandering past the front of the house, unable to take their eyes off him. By the time he had finished, the sweat was pouring off him, and a decent fan base had accumulated at the bottom of the road. To me, it sounded a bit like a Coca-Cola advert.

In the four weeks, Dan was home, we all enjoyed each other's company. We did things together, from walking the dog, Ellie, each day over the moors to creating a fabulous garden. From then on, we have used it whenever we could. Dan also decided he needed to know some basic cooking skills. So in my spare time, I set about teaching him the basics. We started with some essential dishes like Chilli con Carne and Bolognese and gradually moved to a curry. The only thing he could not get his head around was an omelette, and may I add; he still can't. Time rolled on; eventually, Dan received an email to let him know it was time to return to Lympstone to continue his training.

BACK IN TRAINING

Before returning to Lympstone, Dan had to have a PCR test to confirm he was Covid free. Dan had received information concerning bubbles, etc.; they were confined to their landing area and could exercise within their bubble. They had to head to the galley at a specific time for food, and all troop members wore the same coloured wristband, making it easy for the training teams to stop troops mingling together. They were also issued with military face masks, and finally, they were not allowed off camp, except for running as a troop.

Dan returned to Lympstone on Friday, a public holiday commemorating the 75th anniversary of V.E. day. There was a three-week buffer to get the recruits back up to their original fitness. Most of this took place on the bottom field, but they could venture out of the front gates for a run as they were training for the week 15 speed march. It would mark a turning point in the training calendar; if they passed the speed march, they were presented with a green belt signifying commando training was well underway. The next goal would be week 26, when they would be presented with a cap comforter marking the last stage of training.

The recruits were also measured for their lovat and blues uniforms in preparation for passing out.

Dan said just by being measured up for his pass-out uniform gave him a sense of pride and determination all of its own to complete the journey. It was a nod in the right direction since they felt you were capable enough to be measured up for your pass-out uniform.

With Covid 19, most civilian staff who worked in the NAAFI and Laundry were sent home. Therefore, the recruits are now back to handwashing and using drying rooms to clean their kit. During this time, I started sending Dan boxes of his favourite foods. Especially crisps and snacky things as everything was closed and they were not allowed off camp.

I had to send his seventeenth birthday presents this way too. We sent him some North Face flip-flops. They use this kind of slider all the time, perfect for shower runs and grots. They let their feet breathe and heal after exercise in the field as well.

On week 15, they have a drill inspection and an arms drill pass out, which marks the end of phase one.

Phase two teaches the recruit the tactical skills and knowledge required to act as a rifleman in all war operations and the traditional phase of war.

Dan said he loved this part of training. He had mortar training, tactical field patrols, and harbour drills. Starting with a four-mile speed run in the morning, followed by bottom field pass-out practice for week 20. They also did a lot of field exercises as a troop and honed their outdoor skills.

Dan rang one evening and told us about building an observation post at the side of a path. The hole had to be large enough to accommodate four recruits lying down with room to turn. Then they covered it with a roof that appeared natural in the landscape. They used their ponchos to line the hole and used branches and large clumps of heather for the natural look.

One of the recruits kept a record of anything and everything that passed their observation post. They were in the hole for twenty-nine hours. Everything was done in the hole. Dan said the smell was horrendous. They had to eat their rations cold and could not make a sound.

On several occasions, dogs and children walked over the roof and nearly brought it down. They put their legs in the air to hold it up. One dog cocked his leg at the side of the hole, and gradually a trickle of warm liquid enveloped the recipients inside it. Dan said one dog poked his head through the slit where all the observations were being carried out and started growling. The owner, thinking the dog had seen a rabbit, quickly clipped him back on the lead and dragged the poor dog away. He was unaware that four recruits were killing themselves, silently laughing inside the hole. A rabbit visited during the night took one look and scuttled off in another direction.

About 3.30 am, they heard footsteps heading towards them. All four were on high alert. It appears it is another recruit on his first navigational exercise. He slowly comes past, dragging his feet along the ground. He stops and gets out his coordinates all the time chattering away to himself. The lads in the hole are all doing their utmost to contain themselves. They send a message up the line via the radio to warn others in the troop of the intruder.

He marched off, oblivious to the thirty strong recruits watching him, and unbeknown to him, he was the highlight of the evening.

As week 19 reared its ugly head, the bottom field pass-out sorted the men from the boys. Dan rang us, feeling optimistic about the week ahead. As of Monday, it was crash week; it was the last week before the bottom field pass out. To ensure they were ready for the pass out, they were put through their paces every day. They put their bodies through a series of exercises, and as each day dawned, their aches and pains got more intense. They constantly used rollers to ease their muscle pain. I felt exhausted just listening to the details of that day.

Dan explained he would need to complete intensive daily doses of carries, high ropes, and obstacles. Each session is an examination of the recruit's strength and determination; this becomes apparent on the fifth lap of the assault course.

He had been instilled with a new ethos, 'Train hard, fight easy' repeating the intensity of the training makes it familiar and results in the actual test feeling easy. Or so they say.

Each day the recruits try to beat their time from the day before. So by the day of the test, it should feel like a breeze. As week 20 arrives, and this is the one thing on Dan's mind, and although he passed it with ease, failure is just a foot slip or a lack of grip away. A couple of recruits have already had to forgo the pass-out due to injury.

Dan said it started at 11.00 am. He was one of the first to start. With 21lbs in his daysack and a rifle, Dan set off doing a thirty-foot rope climb followed by the assault course, twelve obstacles in five minutes. He lifted another recruit carrying 21lbs and a rifle for 200 metres in a fireman's lift. Then he has the full regain, which is over the infamous water tank. Dan admits it took him a while to gain the measure of the regain. He had realised it's about technique, not strength. You had to pull yourself along a rope halfway, then drop. Then, holding on with your hands, you need to pull yourself back onto the rope. To get to the end, you have to keep moving forward using your leg as a lever on the rope. When this is complete, the torture is over. A couple of lads had ended up in the tank, so they would have to try it again the following day.

All too soon, the following day arrived for the recruits to try once more to conquer the bottom field. All the lads ran down to give them moral support as they are now a close-knit group, and failure wasn't on the cards for any of them. All of them pass out, and the troop lives to fight another day.

The first couple of weeks of lockdown were very surreal. Jon and I would walk Ellie in the morning, and all you could hear were the birds singing and the sheep bleating in the fields. There were no car engines, no screeching brakes, nor constant rumbles as each hour rolled by. The sky was clear of clouds and pollution. The air smelled sweeter from all the flowers in bloom. I thought about my grandparents and what they would have made of all this. It also crossed my mind about the past and wondering if life would have been like at the turn of the century—the quietness and naturalness of the world that was now in limbo.

There was a continuous procession of people walking here and walking there, keeping themselves to themselves for fear of catching the dreaded disease. Nobody knew at this time how it was transmitted or even what it was. Everybody would switch their televisions on in the afternoon to hear the latest news from 10 Downing Street. They would then form an opinion to pass on if anybody asked their thoughts. We were all living from day to day, wondering if life was ever going to be the same.

Thursday at 8.00 pm, we would support our NHS, who had the most challenging time ever. No matter how large, no pay grade could justify what those doctors and nurses endured each day.

The start of June was bizarre. Things were starting to return to a new normal. Wearing a mask was now par for the course if you were going shopping. I think the thing I missed was being able to dine out and meet people. We no longer had any holidays booked. The tour operator had cancelled them all.

Jon and I worked through the first part of lockdown, and now it was slowly easing, and life seemed more precious than it had been before. Seeing people, being able to talk to people seemed such a special thing. Believe it or not, we had learned to live a different way, and it was difficult to change now.

I decided to book a local restaurant for the following Friday. I was looking forward to getting dressed up and seeing how life was beyond the front door. We arrived in good time, and with face masks on, we were escorted to a table for two. As far as the restrictions were concerned at that time, you were allowed to sit down for a meal with your bubble – household, and you had to wear your mask until you were seated.

Not to mention at that time, the death toll was horrific, yet, we were adamant we would stick to the rules. The restaurant soon became packed with parties of 10 and above, and it was apparent they were not family members sitting together. The meal was delicious, and we had enjoyed our outing. Yet, it seemed as though some had decided to continue regardless, giving no thought to the people in the restaurant who were abiding by the rules.

I work in the public sector and have seen how this disease ravaged the country. We were taking away people's livelihoods by not sticking to the rules. We will never overcome Covid if people continue to disbelieve what is in front of them. Many businesses would not withstand another lockdown. I hoped we would all come out the other side appreciating the more minor things in life.

What struck me more than anything is that people made more time for each other. Admittedly we have spoken and had in-depth conversations with our neighbours whom we have only ever said hello to in the past. There is a sense of community now.

It's like the borrowing a cup of sugar from your next-door neighbour kind of feeling; this, I am sure, would have been like the wartime years.

We all found we had one common starting point for a conversation. We were all fearful for the future.

As a result of the constant exercise and sleepless nights, Dan's immune system was weak. If he contracted it, would it affect him differently? Would he become very ill? Worrying times for all of us, that was for sure.

Harris Fitness closed its doors a few months before due to Coronavirus. However, Rob and Emma continued to serve our community. They did it by letting customers borrow equipment and continue classes online. This huge gesture helped so many people in different ways. It brought normality to the day and, to an extent, a purpose to get up for and get moving.

Jon and I were lucky enough to borrow a spin bike for most of the closure. It helped in many ways with our fitness and the social interaction we gained from the Zoom classes.

During the lockdown, little Matilda next door was five years old. Paul and Donna had organised a birthday party which had to be cancelled. Matilda was so upset. Not only had her party been cancelled, but she also couldn't go to school and play with her friends. So Jon and I made her a huge banner and secured it to Paul's fencing. When Matilda awoke on her birthday, she was absolutely amazed.

On V.E. day we organised a street party. Every house on our estate had bunting up. It started pretty calmly.

Gradually as people became more familiar with each other, the fun began.

Dan had to leave that day to travel back to Lympstone, having been home for four weeks. It was the only thing that had happened in lockdown, and typically, he had to leave to continue his training.

We gathered his belongings together, had breakfast then said our goodbyes. I knew that morning I would not be seeing him for a while. It was so tough to see him walk through that door. He blew me a kiss, and then he was gone.

I sat for a while with Ellie's head on my knee and those big brown eyes staring up at me. My big brown bear knew the score by now. She would be my comfort blanket for the next few days until the feeling of loss dissipated. It felt more painful this time around because there was so much sadness everywhere and the fear of the unknown.

Jon arrived home from the train station; he mentioned Dan was the only person in his carriage on the train and the station was empty. He had been tested before travelling, and he would be tested again before he was allowed into the camp.

Putting my thoughts to one side, we put our bunting up and the beers in the fridge and tried to enjoy the rest of the day.

The party carried on into the small hours. The following day everybody seemed to be more upbeat. So, all in all, it had been a worthwhile gathering. We all promised to do the same soon.

As I write this book from the diary I kept about Dan's journey, nothing much has changed one year later. We are due to come out of another lockdown shortly. They say we must start living with it now. We will see.

It was early July, the sun was shining, and we were heading towards the weekend. I was driving back from work thinking about Dan and how long it had been since I had seen him; Jon was off for the weekend, and I had spoken to Dan the night before. They were now able to venture out into Exeter, and I knew he would be going to Exeter at some stage on Saturday.

I spoke with Jon, and we decided to surprise him. So I booked a hotel for Saturday night, and we packed an overnight bag. I knew these next few weeks in his training would be absolute stinkers, so a bit of moral support from Mum and Dad would not harm.

We set off in the early hours, the roads were quiet, and we made decent headway. We stopped at the usual services for a quick coffee and arrived in Exeter about 8.30 am. We wandered around Exeter for a short while, recognising the local pub Dan had mentioned so many times. We took a picture of the pub and told him we were waiting for him.

Within seconds, a text came back asking, 'How have you got a picture of the local pub?' He thought we had photoshopped it. We sent another text with Jon in the picture outside the pub. At last, the penny dropped. He had the quickest shower ever and caught the next train to Exeter. He was so pleased to see us. He couldn't believe we had driven all that way to spend the shortest amount of time with him. Believe me; it was worth it. We ordered breakfast and planned our day. We caught up on all the things he had been doing. He looked different again, with his hair lightened from the sun and a deep tan. His voice had deepened, and there was a maturity about him I had not seen before.

The day passed us by so quickly. We were introduced to most of his troop and enjoyed a tipple with them in the pub we had met Dan in earlier. We made our way to the hotel near Lympstone, unpacked, and had an early dinner before taking Dan back to base. He had to be back for an 8.00 pm landing call.

We agreed to pick him up at 9.30 am for breakfast before our long journey home. Jon took him back to camp. He returned to find me in the bar having a well-deserved glass of wine.

The following morning I woke up early. I was eager to make tracks, pick Dan up, and spend as much time with him as possible before having to make the six-hour journey home.

Jon and I could see him coming across the bridge and entering the car park. Dan jumped in the car, and we set off in search of a big breakfast.

We went to the local farm shop near the base; the restaurant had a wide range of early morning sundries and cooked items. Dan had said hello and shook hands with a lad he knew from his troop. As we were waiting to be seated, the young man made a beeline for Jon shaking his hand. He said what a good lad his son was and what a credit he was to us.

I could hardly contain the pride that rose from the pit of my stomach. At the same time, Jon was beside himself as the tears began to roll from his eyes. Dan berated his dad for being so soft, but you could see his dad's reaction touched him.

We sat by the window; a light breeze came through the open door, and Dan and Jon ordered an enormous breakfast. Dan reviewed the exercise he had been doing the previous week while we waited for breakfast to arrive.

They had been on Second Empire. It was a particularly challenging exercise that involved section attacks, reconnaissance patrols of enemy positions, and creating observation points to observe the enemy. It all culminated in a night attack on enemy positions. Dan loved this side of military life. His face lit up, and the enthusiasm he showed wrapped around us both. Jon and I knew he had made the right decision as far as his career was concerned. I couldn't imagine him ever finding anything else that suited him as well.

Dan paid for breakfast, which I still can't get my head around; my son had money in his wallet and treated his parents to breakfast at such a young age. Most of the recruit's spent their money on food. He used the galley three times a day but found it wasn't enough to keep the hunger at bay.

We made our way back to Lympstone. We all got out of the car, he gave me a hug that made me hold my breath, and I didn't want it to end. A hug that you remember for weeks to come. All Dan said was, 'Thanks, Mum, for coming down. It means a lot.'

We watched him disappear into camp and took the memories with us of a short but needed weekend together. The journey home was quiet—each of us with our thoughts on the past, present, and the future.

I am a glass-half-full kind of girl, so my thoughts were firmly on the future, and the day he would finally pass out. He had just ten weeks of his training left. He was, in effect, two-thirds of the way there. If Covid 19 hadn't reared its ugly head, he probably would just be passing out round about this time.

Over the weekend, we discussed which Commando unit he would like to belong to when he passed out. He had not yet decided, as each unit had their own role to play in the corps.

During lectures, they are taught about the different units and what each unit specialises in so they can choose the unit that suits them best. Each recruit must write down their three top choices just before taking their commando tests. When the tests are complete, they are informed which unit they will be assigned to do their basic Marine training. Basic marine training lasts two years. After this, Dan said they could then train in specific areas.

The weekend had lightened Dan's mood, and seeing us so supportive and mindfully willing him on had given him the determination to get through the next round of training.

During this part of training, week 22, adventure training usually takes place. Some time to relax and take stock; have fun together as a troop surfing, mountain climbing, and sea kayaking.

Due to the Covid situation, the training team was advised to continue the course as nobody knew whether there could be another lockdown.

MIND OVER MATTER

So, on they went onto Violent Entry. Dan knew this exercise was going to be the biggest yet. The exercise was to take place in South Wales in the Brecon Beacons, a place called Sennybridge. He rang one last time, his bergen was packed, and he was ready to go.

Every time Dan is on an exercise, I start counting down the days, but at the same time, I also wish my life away. I didn't want to hear from him until the exercise was complete. If I did, that would mean he had failed the exercise and would be back trooped. So actually, I was in a no-win situation until he had completed the activity and was home safely.

I looked back at the diary I keep; you can see the momentum growing with each exercise. Then, after being taught something, the troop performs a more intense practical than the last time. This is the second to last exercise of training, so it will be intense. I know Dan will give 100%. Whether that is enough is another story.

Seven slow, arduous days later. I received a text saying Dan is back safe and will ring when he can. He had to de-service all the equipment he took on exercise and his uniform; we would not hear from him until it was complete.

Late into the evening, the phone rang. It was Dan, and the first words out of his mouth were that it had been horrendous.

They had set off at around 5.00 pm in the evening and arrived at the destination at about 11.00 pm. Dan was issued with his ammunition and set off on an insertion yomp. Dan said that this week was a stern test of everything they had learned so far. He also explained what was meant by a yomp. The recruits would walk at a fast pace uphill and run downhill. It was very demanding, both physically and mentally.

The sergeant had told them to ditch their bergens and put what they thought they would need in their daysacks for a couple of days. They were also instructed to take the exercise seriously and to play it out as realistically as possible. Dan followed the order, daysack on his back, and they were off. He said they yomped for nearly seven hours each day, culminating in very little skin left on the soles of his feet.

Dan said the final attack was incredible. They had to do a recce of the village where the last attack would take place. Having surveyed their objectives, the troop moved into position and waited until darkness fell before clearing the first buildings quietly. All this is done with the use of night-vision goggles.

The third building had several small rooms to clear. Dans section moved through the ground floor rooms. Then made their way upstairs. They burst in through the door, and out of the corner of Dan's night vision goggles, he saw something move. Before he could turn, the enemy had grabbed him by his leg. To free himself from the enemy's grip, he used the butt of the gun he was carrying to fight the assailant off and free his leg. Then he promptly released a couple of rounds to secure his freedom. Gutsy move considering it was a member of the training team, and Dan had sent him off carrying a black eye.

Dan said by the time the enemy was even aware of them, fire support had already trained their sights on each threat, waiting for the signal to neutralise them. All of a sudden it became very noisy. The mortars, grenades, and explosive entrance charges were more than enough to keep the enemy at bay. Dan and his section kept the momentum going until they had gained a solid foothold.

The next challenge they faced was to hold their ground and push forward into the rest of the village. By day, he said they patrolled the area to suppress enemy activity. They were besieged by the enemy during the night, who tried to break down the defences that they had built in the house they now occupied. Eventually, the enemy broke through their defences and could be heard on the ground floor. They withdrew further up the stairs. As the enemy attempted to gain a foothold on the stairs, they were down rained upon with all the section could muster.

After they dispelled the enemy, they cleared any remaining pockets of resistance left in the village. The next step was to remove all the surrounding areas around the village. Dan explained they had to dig into battle trenches to defend themselves against any follow-up threats. That day he said, was so hot, and by this time, they had not had any sleep and had lived purely on adrenaline and the odd mouthful of water.

Having survived several gas attacks, the next step was to advance to a neighbouring village 10 miles away, and so began the final yomp, or so he thought. They were carrying 40lbs for five/six hours over densely vegetated terrain with steady inclines of over 300 metres. In some areas, they were on their hands and knees, crawling up gradients of 45 degrees.

Dan said they eventually arrived, tormented by the sergeant saying it was just over the next hill. Six hills later, they entered a woodblock. From there, they prepared for their final assault. Following a recce and reconnaissance once more, they were ready to attack. In response to the attack becoming noisy, heavy weapons were employed to take the village. Within minutes the enemy had been dispelled from Wales.

Dan's troops had gathered in one of the evacuated houses to have something to eat and talk about the battle they had just undergone. It was a feeling of pure exhilaration combined with exhaustion. The sergeant from the training team entered and asked the lads to get ready for another yomp. He explained the exercise was not over. If anybody could not carry on, they could step forward and speak with him in the next room.

Dan said there was sheer silence while the lads dealt with the fact they had yet more to do. Dan's feet were in ribbons. Just the fact he would have to put pressure on the base of his feet brought tears to his eyes. Every bone in his body felt ravaged. Dan sat and weighed up the pros and cons. If Dan disclosed he didn't think he would make the next yomp, he would be back trooped and have to do it all again. No brainer, really. He gathered his belongings and shared his thoughts with his section. Despite a few being more severe than him, they all left the building and prepared for the next yomp. Nobody wanted to see the sergeant. They all dug deep and decided they probably could not feel any worse, and it was only pain. The entire training team gathered outside to help the recruits with their bergens, trying to make light of the yomp ahead.

Dan said they started at a swift pace. He could feel the skin on his little toe rubbing against his boot. His shoulders were on fire. Even though he was almost delirious from lack of sleep, he kept moving, concentrating on putting one foot in front of the other. They had been yomping for about five minutes when he saw in the distance a vast hill (which in his mind's eye was Everest) looming in front of him. Dan knew it would take all his strength. Suddenly, his mind turned to the real reason he was suffering. All the blood, sweat, and tears he had already put into his dream had come to the fore, and a wave of determination like no other swept over him. It carried him up the hill where it levelled out. The training team stopped the troops and congratulated them for not giving up. It had been a test to see if, despite the pain and exhaustion, they would carry on and complete the task.

In the distance, they could see the coach making its way through the countryside towards them. Dan felt quite emotional knowing he had completed one of the most horrendous yet amazing things ever. The training staff handed out Mars bars and water to keep the recruits motivated, and within five minutes of them boarding the coach, not a sound could be heard.

Having de-serviced their equipment and a decent night's sleep, the horrors of the past week became a distant memory. Even though their bodies were telling them otherwise, morale was high.

They were due some downtime, so Exeter it was. All the food he had drooled over in his thoughts on the several yomps he had endured in the last week was about to become a reality. Several chicken burgers later, he sat outside the local pub that the lads frequented, having a hearty laugh over their exploits.

The weekend flew by and Monday morning dawned. The lads were heading to Woodbury Common to acquaint themselves with the endurance course. The endurance course is one of the last four tests in commando training. The last time they had seen this was on their PRMC (Potential Royal Marine Course). The lads ran the course in slow time to familiarise themselves with the task ahead. After practising the course as a section, they would then run it individually based on their ability level under the stopwatch.

The endurance course had lots of small, dark, pitched tunnels which the lads had to navigate through; Peters Pool, which is always cold, the Sheep Dip and lots and lots of mud. Dan said the lads couldn't understand where the mud came from as it hadn't rained in weeks, and it was boiling hot, approximately 27 degrees. Dan had a quick water break then headed for a four-mile run back to base. The first mile was through Woodbury Common, which was rough terrain, and then onto some small back roads. The PT led the troop, and Dan thought he was trying to break the land speed record. He was pushing a seven-minute mile pace throughout the run. This would be the first of several visits to Woodbury Common in the next few weeks as the endurance test figures highly in the commando phase. They arrive back at base for a quick change out of the muddy rig and then onto lectures.

Later that week, they had the opportunity to acquaint themselves with The Tarzan Assault Course. Dan loved it. He relayed all of it back to us, saying you had to be fast and agile, and reminded us that the troops had to wear webbing and carry rifles. When Dan got in touch with us the following evening, he explained he had his 12-mile load carry the following day. The load is a little over 69 lb between his bergen and his webbing. This is a load that must be carried 12 miles in the heat of summer.

We invigorate and commiserate all in the same conversation. My heart cries out to him. Dan will put in 100% as always and more if needed. He can actually see the finish line. His confidence has grown massively since Violent Entry.

Friday morning arrived, and Dan was up at 5.30 am, ready for the 12-mile load carry. Each recruit will have their kit weighed to make sure it is 69lb for the criteria.

They all depart on a coach at 6.30 am, and the idea is they will run back to base. Failure is not on the cards today. The whole troop is determined to pass this. They start the run at 7.00 am. Dan said the pace was brutal but didn't expect anything less. He moved into his usual middle of the pack place. Never too fast, never too slow. Among the lads, the motto is 75 stay alive. In civilian terms, it means don't give your all, all the time. You never know when you may need that other 25%. Choose your battles wisely where your energy is concerned.

By 11.15 am, they had all completed the run and headed to the galley for a well-deserved lunch.

The following day they practice night beach landings near Poole. Another box ticked and another week completed.

Monday heralded week 26. But first, some downtime in Exeter with the boys. Dan usually made the journey purely for a change of food and good company and being so young; he found watching the lads chatting up the girls and listening to the banter passed between them funny. Even funnier when they are rebuffed by the female in question.

They eventually returned to base. By this time, some of the recruits are worse for wear. This is where Dan comes into play. Being the only sober recruit in the troop, he makes sure the lads make it to bed without injury or destruction of military property. He had, in the past, cleaned up sick from the bathrooms out of fear of retribution from the training team. The following day, the guilty party always thanked him profusely. I think every troop needs a Dan to watch their back.

Sundays became lazy days. Dan always rang late afternoon, having had a decent lie-in. He usually used this time to get his uniforms ready for the coming week.

It was a big day the following day. If they completed the six-mile speed march in the time allocated, they would forgo the blue beret and receive a 'cap comforter', which would be awarded to them after the run. This represents the start of the commando phase. The comforter was initially worn as a field headdress in the war and is every recruit's dream. Dan had spoken about this hat several times. He had the belt; now he wanted the hat.

Dan got up early that morning, and I sent him a message letting him know we would be thinking about him on his six-mile run and asked him to send us a photo of him wearing his hat. The reply back was, 'A piece of cake, this one, Mum'.

Jon and I had decided to have a couple of days away in York. The restrictions caused by the lockdown had been lifted as far as travel was concerned, so I had booked a two-night stay. This was likely to be the only break we would have in quite some time.

We'd set off early to make the most of the beautiful sunshine. Two hours later, we were checking into our room in a beautiful hotel on the outskirts of York. We quickly unpacked and made our way out into the glorious sunshine. We walked up through the city gates and headed for a bar down by the river. It was table service due to Covid 19, the waitress came to take our order, the wine arrived, and it was time to relax and enjoy.

Well into my second glass of wine, my phone started ringing. I looked at the number but didn't recognise it. I answered, not expecting what I was about to hear.

Dan's commanding officer was on the other end of the phone. He explained that on the six-mile run, Dan had collapsed with heatstroke. They had managed to get him back to the med bay and plunged him into an ice bath to try and cool his body down just in the nick of time. His internal organs had started to shut down due to his internal temperature. They were now running tests, and he would most certainly have damaged his internal organs, but they didn't know how severe. He had lost consciousness at one stage. If it hadn't been for the quick-thinking actions of the training team and being so close to the base, I don't think Dan would be with us today.

I asked what would happen next. He couldn't give me those answers at this early stage. However, he said the troop was gutted for him. He would be missed by them all, including the training team. They were still holding out that he would continue his training with their troop, but as every hour ticked by, the light dimmed on that happening.

He continued to say Dan had literally been 50 metres from finishing when he had collapsed and that Dan had given it everything he had. Two members of the training team were running with him, realising he was struggling, which was unusual for him. They managed to catch him as he fell.

His training officer said he was conscious and could I ring him for moral support, as he was physically and mentally in lousy shape. I finished speaking to Dan's commanding officer and relayed what had been said to Jon. He looked so deflated and was utterly lost for words and was looking at me for answers. I had none.

With tears springing up in all directions, we ordered another drink and contemplated our next move. I regained my composure. I couldn't even think about what could have happened. I would deal with my thoughts on that later. I needed to focus on just what was happening at that moment. A hearty slurp of wine, and I was now ready to deal with what was to come.

We moved somewhere slightly quieter and dialled Dan's number. He picked up almost straight away. I wanted to ask how he was, but it sounded like such a stupid question. All I could do was reassure him it was a setback but not the end of his dream. I knew Dan would react differently if he knew we were upset. So the most effective course of action was to act indifferently. He was really upset about not getting his cap comforter. He had based the last eleven weeks on a challenging, gut-wrenching exercise to achieve this next goal.

We calmed him down, and he began to realise it wasn't the end of the world. The doctor explained that he was a lucky lad and that it could have played out so differently. If he hadn't been so close to the base and the training team hadn't reacted so quickly. We could have been looking at a fatality.

He was to stay in Med Bay until his blood results came back. They would then evaluate and see what treatment was required, but he was looking at considerable time off.

To reiterate, I asked him not to jump to conclusions and to wait and see. I promised to call him later.

Jon and I didn't know what to do, whether to return home or wait and see what would happen.

We had lunch and wandered the Shambles, not really taking in the sites. It gave me breathing space to take in what had just happened and how close we had been to losing our precious son.

We made our way back to the hotel, both with our own thoughts. It had not been a good day.

As we were climbing the stairs to our hotel room, I heard a ping from my phone. I grabbed my phone, thinking it was a message from work. It wasn't. It was a picture of Dan with a cap comforter on sporting a massive grin on his face.

The phone rang, and he explained the CSM had visited him and congratulated him on actually completing the six-mile run. He said the finish line was six miles and 500 metres, so strictly speaking, he met the criteria and awarded him his cap. He also told him he would make it. He had what it took to be a Royal Marine Commando and that his troop would miss him. Just those few words made all the difference to him. So an unfortunate situation had now been turned on its head by someone going out of their way to assure a young lad with a big dream, it was still achievable. It just may take a little longer.

Dan stopped in Med Bay for the rest of the week. His blood tests showed his internal organs were returning to normal. The doctor was amazed at how quickly they were healing, and within a week, his blood tests were coming back as normal. So no lasting damage, which we were all thankful for under the circumstances.

Dan's mood was up and down over the next week. He was once again in limbo. Not knowing how long it would take to get back on his feet. The first prediction was six months rest and recovery, but seeing how Dan had bounced back, that time had been severely reduced. Lympstone was closing for the summer in a week, so Dan would be home very soon anyway.

He called to say the doctor had given him the all-clear to travel home. Dan also said he was on medication but was fine to catch the train. He would be home for a month, and in that time, we would make sure we rebuilt his fitness and well-being.

I wasn't concerned about how things affected him mentally. I was worried about Dan's approach to setbacks, which he classified as failures. Dan needed to revert his way of thinking. He was going through a difficult time and was so young that any setbacks were viewed as failures. We needed to change that mindset.

THE ROAD TO RECOVERY

We arrived at the train station to collect Dan from the scheduled train on platform five. I spotted him grappling with a bag and sent Jon over to help him. By this time, the holdall was slung over his shoulder, and he was heading towards us. He looked very pale and tired. A huge smile covered my face, along with the cursory gulp in the back of my throat. He gave me a Royal Marine hug which was so tight it drew the air out of my lungs, and he kissed me on the cheek.

We headed towards the car. As part of his training, he was made aware that being in the military, specifically the Marines, he needs to be mindful of his surroundings and potential threats that may be there. His eyes were everywhere, and he did not settle until we were home.

Gradually, the layers started to come off over the next few days, and he began to relax. On one afternoon, he relived his latest ordeal to both of us.

It had been like any other morning. Up at 5.30 am, shower, breakfast, and ready to start the run at 7.00 am before it got too hot. He had done the run several times in the last couple of weeks, and it hadn't been a problem. He felt relaxed when he started; the PT instructor had set a fast pace, but he thought it was manageable. Coming up to the fifth mile, he began to take his foot off the peddle. His body was beginning to hurt. He carried on but slowly was being overtaken by the other lads in the troop. He tried to speed up, but more lads passed him. He was confused. Why was he running? Who were all these people? Two of his training team were next to him, asking him if he was OK. They were trying to encourage him. He could hear the lads calling his name from the finish line—just a few more steps and then nothing.

He remembered being plunged into the ice bath but very little else. The next thing he remembered was people asking him questions which he couldn't answer. He was confused. He didn't know who he was and why he was there. Very slowly, things began to become a little clearer. The doctor explained to him what had happened and that he had been very fortunate.

As with most things he's endured, he took the event well, but it's the back troop that doesn't sit right with him. He feels he will have to prove himself once more and fit into an already established troop. Over the next week, we have several conversations about back trooping. We explain that is the way it is, and he will have to deal with change constantly at short notice as a Royal Marine and that plans, more often than not, do not go to plan.

Jon and I decide to throw him a surprise party in the garden, which was allowed with the change in Covid restrictions. This was to celebrate his birthday but also to show Dan how proud people were of him. I think he needed this more than anything. His friends let him know how well he had done so far, and the adults conveyed their confidence that he would make it.

Dan stopped at a friend's the night before and had no idea the party was the next day. The weather looked unpredictable, so my faithful friend was there to lend a hand. Janice appeared with a gazebo. It was like trying to complete a giant jigsaw, but with the help of Janice's husband Mike, we managed to erect it before darkness fell.

The following morning we were up early to prepare the food ready for the BBQ. Cupcakes next and Eton mess, and we were all set. Jon had put bunting right around the garden in Royal Marine green. The scene was set; all we needed were the guests and the leading man.

People had begun to gather in our garden, including his school friends. People had made a special effort to wish him well. Joanne had arrived earlier with another close friend Sue, and laden with prosecco and nibbles, they settled themselves down for an afternoon of laughter. It was really lovely to see Katie, Dan's old pastoral coordinator from school. She had supported Dan and me through the process and kept in touch since Dan had left Ribblesdale. I knew her opinion mattered to him. Two other significant people arrived; they were his two older stepbrothers who had supported him from the shadows—always being on hand when he needed to talk.

A text arrived, letting me know he was on his way. I watched the car come down the road. He climbed out and headed towards the gate to the garden—everyone was in complete silence. The gate opened, and a huge cheer erupted to welcome him to his own party.

He was utterly gobsmacked and overwhelmed. I knew we had made the right decision to have the party by the sheer delight on his face.

The party went on all afternoon and into the early evening. The weather had been kind and kept dry. The fire pit we had built into the patio was being looked after by Jon and a team of helpers. Sausages and burgers were cooked to perfection and handed out in brioche buns. Jon had built some pull-up bars in the garden for Dan. Of course, they were a hit, with lads showing off in front of their girlfriends. Competitions were won and lost. Joanne even ventured onto the bars at one stage, and I do believe everyone had a brilliant day. For most people, this would have been the first time they had mixed with families other than their own for months. I think it lifted everyone's spirits. They laughed and joked, and they shared their experiences of the last six months of lockdown, realising how much they missed conversation and company, which was a fantastic outcome.

Over the next few days, Dan returned to the Harris fitness gym. This was because they had recently been able to reopen after a substantial closure from Covid 19. Rob always had a lot of time for Dan. He, more than most, realised how much effort is involved in training to be a Royal Marine and supported Dan through the process. Like many others, he wanted him to succeed.

Dan had a strict regime to stick to. It was essential to run on the treadmill with a twenty-five-kilogram weight vest. He pushed himself continually to return to optimum fitness.

The lads from his (now) old troop kept in touch with the sergeant, who rung him a couple of times to see how he was and filled him with confidence in his ability. This gave him a real boost. He was itching to return and resume his training.

At the beginning of September, Dan returned to Lympstone. We packed most of his clothes the night before, so a leisurely morning was spent talking to friends and saying his goodbyes. His PCR test came back negative, so he was good to go. They say if you do something repetitively, it becomes easier. May I say, watching my son walk through the front door doesn't get any easier. Because of his setbacks, it makes it much more challenging. I know I cannot protect him, and he must make his own mistakes and learn to deal with them. Whatever they may be.

Dan rang to let me know he had arrived, and his lateral flow was negative. Until he could move the next day, he was still with his old troop. The troop and the training team were pleased to see him back. The sergeant gave him a pep talk and told him that he would be wearing the coveted green beret, in no uncertain terms, before he knew it.

The following day, he moved to Hunter company, it was until he felt 100% and was cleared by the doctor. He was now chomping at the bit and wanted to just crack on and get the last six weeks under his belt. Dan maintained his focus on the end goal. He is moved to Stig (the short-term injury group). He could be found most days on the bottom field. One particular day, the PT instructor called him over to ask him if he had suffered an injury to his right foot as he was running with a limp. It wasn't significant, but it was there. Dan said he was unaware of it. The instructor told him he would refer him to the doctor. So they could have a look at his foot. The doctor confirmed the observation of the PT instructor. He thought it had probably been made by the boot originally. He also asked Dan what state his feet were in after each exercise. Dan told him that his feet were horrendous after each exercise. The doctor recommended a lighter boot to be worn that was vented. Dan picked the lightweight boots up from the stores; they were so much more comfortable, and Dan said it was like walking on air.

A month or so later, Dan received the all-clear from the doctor and joined his next troop. He moved all his gear over on Friday and spent the weekend getting to know his new roommates.

Monday was the six-mile speed march that had nearly killed him. He already had his cap comforter, so there was no real need to do the run, but Dan had other ideas; he wanted to do the run to prove to himself and his new troop that he was worthy of wearing it.

As usual, the troop set off at a fast pace. Dan continued to stay up near the front. At no stage did he feel fatigued and completed the run in good time. His confidence skyrocketed after this result. He could now wear his cap comforter with pride, knowing he had earned it fair and square.

The rest of the day was spent preparing for an exercise called Foggintor. Dan said this consisted of abseiling with and without a fully packed bergen. Dan said it was more complex than it sounded. He said the troop would be introduced to river crossings with bergen attached, and the water was freezing. This gave them an insight into what was to come as the nights were drawing in and getting colder.

They were up bright and early the following day. They headed by coach to Foggintor Quarry with the mountain leaders. During the day, the troop took part in several cliff assaults and climbs with and without their kit. Dan explained they used numerous techniques and equipment supplied by the mountain leaders.

Of course, they left the best for last. It is the beginning of November. The soldiers are instructed to strip naked and change into their full Gortex clothing with just their trainers. The first lad hooked his bergen onto the line that stretched across the quarry basin, which has slowly filled with water over time. He pushed the bergen along the rope and swam simultaneously until he got to the other side. He could then change clothes again. Not a very pleasant experience but a great learning curve. Dan said they had also learned different techniques that the Royal Marines use for assaults and getting over difficult obstacles in obscure places.

We spoke to Dan in the early evening. They were all preparing for Final X. This is the last exercise before they do their commando tests. They must complete this test, and the result is a pass or fail. A lot of recruits drop out of this exercise because it is so exhausting. In this exercise, you are expected to apply all the knowledge and skills you have been taught. You are also expected to show the training team you can perform to a Royal Marine standard.

I could feel the apprehension in his voice. I could also sense the excitement. He face-timed me to show me what his bergen looked like with a part for a rocket launcher tucked into the back. It weighed just over 65lbs. It was Thursday. Dan said if we hadn't heard from him by Monday, he had made it. They had a brief not long before they set off, explaining the objectives of the exercise:

The first mission was to take over a farmhouse before nightfall, with all troop sections getting involved. They would then find a safe harbour for the remainder of the night. Two sections of the troop would carry out ambush raids on known enemy positions throughout the night.

The following day the recruits were given details of the next task. In the absence of sleep, they embarked on their biggest yomp yet. After yomping for most of the day, they arrived at the harbour destination. From there, they orchestrated different attacks, with each section rotating through the different roles of assault, fire support, and support. The attacks became swifter and more precise, with sections communicating more effectively with each other and the commanding officer.

They lost three days in section attacks, with very little sleep, but their confidence was climbing.

Sunday morning was the start of the dreaded killer yomp. This yomp is remembered in Nod law as the Nod slayer. This yomp separates the professionals from the amateurs. A 22km climb over Dartmoor and an unforgiving landscape make it live up to its name. Missteps result in broken bones and torn ligaments. Some troops have taken thirteen to fourteen hours to arrive at their destination. The troop suffered two casualties along the way but arrived in good time. When they arrived, the training team distributed chocolate and drinks, which Dan said tasted marvellous. Dan said somehow it had made the yomp worthwhile just for that taste of sweetness in his mouth. He was not familiar with the recruits in this troop but had seen and spoken to a few of them in the past. Dan described this one young lad who was at the back and struggling to keep the torturous pace of the yomp. Dan slowed down and waited for the young lad to catch him up. He paced him back into the troop and kept his mind busy reciting the menu of a famous takeaway. Soon they were over the initial setback, and the young lad had regained his confidence and composure and was back in the game. He thanked Dan for his help and returned to his section with renewed vigour.

Dan was exhausted, as was everybody else. He had landed a couple of times awkwardly on his right foot and could feel a sharp pain running up the back of his ankle. No way was Dan taking his boot off until he was safely back at camp. His boot was now supporting his ankle, and he eliminated the pain from his mind.

After some more section and troop attacks, it was time to leave Dartmoor and prepare for the final attack. First, they performed a cliff assault. It involved working with the mountain leaders who put the ropes in place. They were instructed to take out the enemy at Scraesdon Fort, which was built in 1859. The attack took place at night using night-vision goggles. Adrenaline burst out of every pore as the recruits climbed the many steps leading up to and from the catacombs where they had broken into the fort.

They had used all the skills and drills they had been taught. Using their knowledge from previous missions and tasks, they systematically cleared the sections and the different rooms in the fort and finally completed their objectives. It had been a good exercise with the culmination of recruits turning into soldiers.

The week-long exercise had resulted in six casualties and completely exhausted recruits.

On the coach on the way back, the atmosphere was one of triumph. They had all completed the most crucial exercise of all. I don't think many recruits completed without injury. Dan was struggling with his heel, and he had blisters where his bergen had rubbed his back. All the recruits had lost weight. Dan weighed in 5 lbs lighter. He would soon put that back on.

Jon and I knew Dan would be returning from the exercise on Thursday. We just didn't know when he would be able to ring as they had to de-service all their equipment, and we knew he would be shattered.

Busy making tea for the two of us, I hear the sound of a text landing on my phone. My first thought was it was Dan letting me know he was OK and he would ring later when he had time. I was right in thinking it was Dan. It was the message I had got wrong. It read, 'I failed and don't want to talk about it.'

I was in a state of shock and bewilderment. He had been through all that and had failed. It didn't seem fair. Jon was beside himself. I rang Janice to let her know and burst into tears. I could not believe the cruelty of it all. I knew Dan would be absolutely devastated. He would have put 100% in and would have never given up.

I wanted to wrap my arms around my son and tell him everything was going to be okay. That he needed to pick himself up, dust himself down, and get back on that horse. It wasn't the end of the dream; it was just a hiccup. He was young, and he had plenty of time. He just had to hang on in there.

I didn't ring him. I thought it would be prudent to leave him until he had calmed down, had some rest, and was ready to talk.

That night proved to be the longest I have had in a long time. Sleep evaded me that night. I felt angry that someone could be so cruel to my son, and I didn't know how he would come back from this.

At work the following day, I couldn't concentrate. I hoped he felt a little better today and would ring me to discuss what the training team said.

In a lot of ways, I was dreading the call. I was no expert on military matters, but I knew he would be hurting, and I could at least ease the pain a little. I just had to wait for the call.

The call eventually came. Dan was distant. I didn't want to play the harsh love card just yet as I didn't know the full depth of how much had transpired. My heart cried out to him. I could feel his tears rolling down his face. He apologised for letting us down, which I instantly reacted to, and explained he could never let us down.

I asked what had happened, and slowly, he began to explain everything. He had completed the exercise; there was a great feeling of relief among the remaining troops.

They had all got on the coach feeling on top of the world.

They returned to Lympstone by late morning. All the lads were clambering for showers, dealing with wounds, and de-servicing their kit. A training team member asked Dan to go to the office to meet the commanding officer. He said he could feel his stomach drop, and he could feel his hands starting to shake. This was due to the massive surge of adrenalin that had just coursed through his body. He entered the office. All members of the training team had gathered to discuss his performance.

The commanding officer basically told him the training team had not seen enough of him to warrant a pass. With Dan being so young and the training team not knowing his capabilities. Due to joining the troop only two weeks earlier, they all needed to make the right decision. This time around, it was going to be a fail.

Dan said he left the room in a daze. His first thought was he was going to quit, throw in the towel. In his eyes, he had given his all and couldn't give anymore. To him, it wasn't enough. He avoided the grots and went to get some air. He said he felt like a failure and wasn't good enough to be there.

I pointed out that this would be the first time he had failed any of the tests in commando training, and he needed to stop being so hard on himself. I also made him aware that it wasn't a failure; it was a setback. He could overcome it by turning a negative into a positive. He needed to stop feeling so sorry for himself and crack on with the task ahead.

Dan now knew what was required to complete Final X. He now had the knowledge to let it work for him. I then played the tough love card, and it worked. I could start to hear a change in his mood. I changed the subject, and we talked about Christmas, which was only a few weeks away. I ended the call feeling totally pessimistic about the way he had been treated. Any mother would have those same thoughts.

The following morning my negativity had disappeared; my positivity was back. I packed a shoebox of goodies and sent it to Dan. He would receive them the next day—his usual favourites of spicy crisps and chocolate and the essentials, boot polish, and shower gel.

Dan texted me that morning saying he had visited Med Bay and they had been concerned about his Achilles. A boot was placed on it, and it was iced every few hours. The equipment for such injuries is probably the most advanced in the world. He had to return to the med bay to use an electronic icepack several times a day. Amongst his other injuries was the bottom of his back. It had blistered and was now drying out nicely.

The lads from the troop had rallied around Dan. He knew quite a few lads from different troops by now, and everyone felt gutted for him. His sergeant from the previous troop visited him. They had a chat about the training team's decision, and Dan felt a lot better about moving forward. The sergeant from the Netherlands saved the day again. He cannot be named for obvious reasons, but if I ever have the good fortune to meet this remarkable man, the drinks would be on me.

Once more, he would have to move troops. The medical team advised Dan not to rush into another Final X too soon as his body still had scars from the last one. To give him a fighting chance of completing the exercise, he would need time to repair both physically and mentally. They advised him to move into Stig (short-term injury group) for a few weeks to recuperate. Additionally, they gave him a schedule of exercises to perform and advised him to continue carrying light loads whenever possible.

So a plan was put in place, and he was given a start date of the New Year to join his new troop and tackle Final X once more.

I think the sergeant (my saviour), who had visited him, felt that it would be a productive exercise to keep him busy due to his low mood. He asked him to organise and deliver, with the help of some other recruits, meals for the lads who had to isolate due to Covid 19. This kept him busy intermittently throughout the day.

I rang him in the evenings. I don't think he wanted to talk. For most of his training, the lads he had been with had now passed out and were spread across the country. I was genuinely worried about him. So much so that I rang the padre. He put me in touch with family liaisons. This is part of the Royal Marines Charity Organisation. They are amazing. I spoke to a retired Royal Marine. He explained that the training team had probably made a genuine call. There was nothing wrong with his performance. If that were the case, they would have had no hesitation in back trooping him. It was normal for him to feel the way he did in the circumstances. I asked if there was anything I could do to help him. When he was ready to talk, he told me to be there to listen.

I felt a lot better having spoken to someone about how he felt. The hurt Dan felt was real. I didn't know if he had the tools to deal with the disappointment, being so young, or whether he was mature enough to understand and bounce back. Time would tell.

We spoke most evenings. His present troop was now undergoing their commando tests. The first one being the nine-mile run. The troop marched back into camp to rapturous applause.

Dan said he could hear the clapping from his room, so he decided to show his support for his troop. He gathered with a few others to watch them pass by. Dan was happy for them all on the outside, but on the inside, all he could think about was 'that could have been me'. One of the lads from his section winked at him as he passed; he came to find Dan later to reassure him he would be next.

A small act of kindness like that made all the difference at what seemed a really difficult time.

Dan continued with his duties and exercised each day. His Achilles was recovering well with the exercises the physio team had instructed him to do. The swelling had all but disappeared, and he was able to stand on it for longer lengths at a time.

At Lympstone, they have a recreational area where recruits can meet and socialise. There is a small kitchen with tea and coffee making facilities, a pool table, and Xbox. A giant screen is located on one of the walls, and recruits can watch films.

Dan had never used this social area, or should I say he never had time to use it, but he had the chance to spend a great deal of time down there. He found it hard dealing with the excitement and the hustle and bustle of his present troop working through their commando tests and getting ever nearer to completing training. He would be home for Christmas soon. When he returned to Lympstone after Christmas, he would embark on Final X once more. He hoped to have completed his training before February and secured his green lid once and for all.

A GOOD BREAK

As Dan's train travelled up the country to the northwest, Jon was on shift. He took a break from work and drove around to the station to pick him up. Jon took him back to work with him until his shift finished.

Dan made himself at home in Jon's workshop while his dad finished his shift. He had been congratulated on his career path and how well he had done so far by members of his dad's shift. They told him over and over how proud his dad is of him. Dan seems to be taken aback by the number of people that know about him. As his dad explained to him on their way home, people are interested in the difficult path he had taken, and people wanted him to complete his journey.

Jon is quite a solitary person. He struggles to show his feelings, or should I say he doesn't know how to communicate his deepest thoughts. Dan has grown up knowing he is loved by us both. I wear my heart on my sleeve and reassure him continually of my love. His dad is more subtle. Like most men, he assumes Dan knows he loves him and is proud of him. In just this small act,

Dan realises how much he means to his dad. This indirectly motivates Dan to put the past behind him and concentrate on the future. Sometimes we all get consumed by negativity, especially if things aren't working out the way we would like. Just a slight shift in one direction or another can bring back the fighting spirit like no other, and positivity reigns once more.

As Christmas approached, the government eased the lockdown for five days during Christmas. It made very little difference to us, really. We were just grateful Dan was home for Christmas. We had enough food and drink to sink a battleship. People were in good humour, generally, as life would be close to normal over the Christmas period.

Dan spent time with his friends over Christmas. Cameron's family gladly welcomed him into their home. They are interested in his adventures thus far and make light of what Dan would call his failings. If you are in the thick of it at Lympstone, everyone you talk to wants the same thing as you do. It is difficult to switch off from it all. While he was home, Dan could do that. We would take long walks over Wiswell Moor, talking about the past and, of course, the future.

For the first time in years, we had a covering of snow. Up on the moors, it was pretty deep, and Ellie was in her element. She had never played in the snow before. Dan throws a snowball for her, and of course, she dives for it, and it disappears into the landscape. The search then begins to try and find the perfectly shaped ball that just vanished into thin air. A snowball fight started between father and son; Jon hid behind a drystone wall, eagerly constructing snowballs. Occasionally, the top of his head could be seen as he launched an attack on his son. The latter was carrying out similar activities behind a gorse bush. Gradually, Jon was inundated with a bombardment of wet missiles. Dan made a run to overpower his dad behind the wall. The battle draws to a close as dad's head appears and is pounded with arms full of snow. The laughter could be heard through the valley below. All that could be seen were two wet, bedraggled men laughing like small children, followed by a happy chocolate labrador in a similar state.

We walked miles over the Christmas holidays. In all honesty, there was very little else to do. Harris Fitness was closed due to Covid once more. The weather had turned cold, so the snow on the roads and paths was covered with sheet ice. Running was out of the question. Dan had no choice but to exercise at home using his original plan and increasing the intensity of each interval.

Once more, Rob and Emma from Harris Fitness let the members take the equipment from the gym. They continued to motivate and inspire people through their online classes. I greatly admire this couple who have given up so much to help the community through a difficult time. Nothing is too much trouble for them, and they always go above and beyond for their members.

By then, Dan was in a positive place and was looking forward to joining his new troop. We have had long conversations about his training. He revealed to us over the holidays that he slept with one eye open when he first started. He could never sleep through the night without waking, worrying that he had everything for the following day. It was natural, and both Jon and I had been through it when we had started new jobs. He said he still had moments like that, but overall, things had improved dramatically. I explained to Dan that he would move through stages of feeling anxious because his role was constantly evolving. This would be something that would subside as he became more confident in his position.

We also had a conversation about feeling low and mental health-related issues. Dan explained the Corps promoted an open door policy. The recruits had been made aware of the warning signs of mental health issues and about alerting someone about your concerns if you feel someone is suffering. Dan also said the Corps promoted 'lifting the lid', which sends out a powerful message that it was okay to feel like that, and it was okay to ask for help.

I felt so much better knowing he knew about mental health and how it can affect even the strongest people.

That time was drawing near again. Our son was about to return to Lympstone. I knew he was in a far better place now and ready to take on the world. I drove him to the station. We parked in the short-stay car park. We both got out of the car; he gave me the usual bear hug and a kiss on the cheek, and he headed off to check his train time. I sat in the car for a moment or two, watching him disappear into the train station. I had to try and keep myself in check as I could feel the tears forming in the corner of my eyes. A deep breath and a change of thought, and the tears remained in my eyes and didn't come tumbling down.

Ellie was waiting for me when I returned home and remained close for the rest of the day in case I needed a snuggle. Jon rang to make sure all was well and said he would try and get home from work a little earlier than usual.

I busied myself for the rest of the day, and by the time Jon came home, my sadness had left, and positivity had returned.

Dan rang to say he had arrived, and his lateral flow was negative. On the following Wednesday, he would be embarking on Final X with his new troop. His heel had recovered along with his back, and mentally he was in a better place. He had joined a new troop and once again knew a couple of lads in the troop. Dan said they all seemed like nice lads and had welcomed him in. As a result, he was happy to share the positive aspects of Final X with his section. This puts him in a strong position, and his confidence is beginning to grow.

Dan called to let us know that he was due to leave for his second Final X. He seemed nervous, which we expected, but I could also hear a tinge of excitement in his voice. He had always said this is the best part of training, practising what you have been taught. I told him that I loved him and to stay safe. We said our goodbyes, and then he was gone. In situations like that, you always tend to say, 'Good Luck'. In Dan's opinion, saying 'Good Luck' meant the person doesn't think you're up to it, and by throwing the good luck in, it may just help you succeed. So no good luck in our household.

A case of no news is good news once again, and the days drag on slowly. We are once more in lockdown. I usually take Ellie for a walk up towards Wiswell; the small village road leading up to it is busier than usual. They're all trying to fill their day. As each day passes, my stress levels lower. We head into the weekend. The thought of his last Final X keeps my mind occupied.

Would he injure himself this time? Would he come back with the same result as last time? Monday arrived, and still no phone call. This is good, isn't it? Well, actually, it means nothing if last time is anything to go by.

Janice and I were busy at work on Wednesday, organising interviews and staffing kitchens. The time flew past. Thursday, I woke up feeling flustered. That butterfly thing was happening in my stomach. I headed downstairs to be greeted by Ellie; I quickly gave her breakfast, then we were off up the road to Wiswell. As we walked, I asked the man upstairs in the sky to make Dan's day a happy one. It was only a mother's opinion, but I thought he had been through enough, and he has proved his worth many times over.

Lunchtime comes and goes. I can't eat anything. My stomach feels like a washing machine on the spin cycle. A couple of hours tick by; it was around this time last time I received the text. Yet another hour passed. Should I ring him? No, I didn't want to ring him and be faced with bad news again. He might not be ringing because it is bad news. My head is in turmoil.

I decided to take Ellie out for another walk. We had recently discovered a new walk that takes us across fields and up to Wiswell. Ellie is addicted to her ball. You can get her to do anything if you have a ball, or so I thought. We passed through the first gate. I let her off the lead. She was running after her ball when I noticed something moving from the corner of my eye. It was a young deer. I ran to put her on her lead right away. Too late. She had picked up the scent, and she was off. Ellie ran to the bottom of the field. I was now pelting down the field after her. I looked up to find she had disappeared entirely. I caught sight of her running along the hedge line of the next field, trying to find a hole in the edge. The A59 was in the distance, and she was heading straight for it. I called out her name. I screamed, 'I have a biscuit.' Why I thought a biscuit would clinch the deal and she would swiftly return when she had prime venison in her sights, I will never know.

It wasn't long before I spotted her again as she ran along the fence line of the next field, bar one. By then, my legs were stung with nettles, and I had scratches all over the back of them from an unassailable blackberry bush.

I managed to clamber over the fencing and started running in her direction. Ellie spotted me and obviously decided the game was over. She came strolling over like butter wouldn't melt. On the other hand, I looked like I had been dragged through a hedge backwards, which in fact, was nearly correct. All the way home, I mumbled to Ellie how I could do without the hassle, today of all days.

With all this drama raging on, Dan had gone from my mind, but not for long. I returned home to a message on my phone from Dan. I was so pleased to read, 'I think I passed'. Until it was official, I didn't want to jinx it.

Not long after the text, Dan rang. He assumed he had passed as he hadn't been asked to report to and see the commanding officer. He was over the moon. This was a brilliant result. Dan's Achilles had just about held up, but he was in pain. He had an appointment with the doctor the next day. If, for whatever reason, he could not start the commando tests. Guess what? He would have to do

Final X again. I knew, for a fact, that wasn't going to happen.

By this point, the lockdown and Covid 19 have affected everyone in the country. None more so than at Lympstone. The recruits had lateral flow tests twice a week. If a recruit had been home for any length of time, a PCR test was required to travel back.

For the first time since Dan's training started, luck had shone on him. I hated to say this but, someone in his troop tested positive. So they all had to isolate themselves in the grotts for the next ten days. So Dan got his wish and was able to relax and rest his foot, ready for the commando tests.

The training team gave each recruit a plastic bag. In the bags were a green beret and the badge. They were instructed to soak the beret in water, strain the excess water away and mould onto their heads and then leave it to dry. The beret will then be a perfect fit when it has dried. They must also ensure the beret is smooth, so a shaver removes excess strands and fluff from the felt. Then last of all, the badge is pinned to the front. They are told under no circumstances must they wear their berets, as they had not completed the four commando tests, and it was bad luck.

Just this small act has given the lads in the troop a massive morale boost. They are so close now. It is within touching distance.

They were not allowed out of the building for any reason. Food would be shipped in and, any Nod passing the grotts would receive a list and cash to buy chocolate, crisps, and snacks from the NAAFI. If the troop ordered takeaway, the Nods would pick the order up from the main gate and deliver it to the door of the grotts. May I add, this is all for a price, and as the week moves on, the price goes up. They are happy to pay, but the food they receive isn't enough to keep them occupied.

They erect ropes and abseil down the three flights of stairs. They find some boxing gloves and have a boxing match one evening. They watched films and played cards. All Dan's friends and family are bombarded with phone calls to ease the boredom. Finally, the ten days have come to an end.

Dan informed us that he was heading on exercise for a couple of days and would call when he returned. His whole demeanour had changed since passing Final X. He now had the confidence to do anything he put his mind to, including blocking out pain.

The training team explained what would happen when isolation finished. Usually, when the troop had finished Final X, they would go straight into their commando tests. Final X would have exhausted the recruits, but they must give everything they have left to the tests. The recruits have had ten days to recuperate now, so the only fair thing to do would be to take them to Woodbury Common for a two-day exercise to tire them out. The bergens are packed, and they move off.

Dan rang Thursday of that week. He said it had been a tough forty-eight hours, very similar to Final X. No sleep and constantly on the move. His Achilles was giving him a little pain but nothing to worry about.

I assumed the pain was under control, and he wasn't worried about it. The only reason he didn't tell me how severe it was was that he didn't want me to worry or persuade him otherwise.

A medic advised resting it. Dan explained to the medic that it was not possible. The medic, realising how determined this young man was, showed him how to wrap his ankle with tape when starting each commando test. He also prescribed ibuprofen and painkillers to be taken intermittently. The rest was up to Dan. Mind over matter is the terminology for it.

The Commando tests mark the end of training. This intense phase ends with a series of tests, which have virtually remained unchanged since. World War II.

THE COMMANDO TESTS

Saturday morning arrives. The sky is clear, and the frost covers everything in its path. This day marked day one of the commando tests. Dan rang last night to say he was ready for it. I could sense the excitement in his voice. It was very similar to when Dan was sitting his exams. He loved the challenge. This is when Daniel is at his best.

Everybody was nervous, and the atmosphere in the grotts was tense. The lads were up early for breakfast. Silence reigned, each with their own thoughts and coping mechanisms. They headed down to Woodbury Common for the endurance test. Dan would ring as soon as the test was over.

Dan had completed the endurance test several times and had passed with minutes to spare.

We waited all morning for the phone to ring. Eventually, Dan's name became visible on my mobile. I took a deep breath and answered to hear a very excited, happy lad on the phone. Dan had passed.

They had walked the four miles up to Woodbury Common with webbing and the standard-issue SA 80 rifle, which can fire single rounds or bursts. This was used on the 25-metre firing range at the latter stages of the test. The recruit must ensure the rifle doesn't get wet as it may not be serviceable on the range.

It was still dark. The walk up to the Common was quiet. All the lads had different thoughts going through their minds. Some were more nervous than others.

The actual test was a six-mile course. The test had to be completed in seventy-three minutes; it has two miles of tunnels, pipes, wading pools, and an underwater culvert known as the Sheep Dip.

Dan said they then had to run the four miles back to base wet through and full of mud, having got through all the tunnels. Dan said he had struggled at this point but kept pushing on. He seemed to have no energy. His chest was burning, and it was difficult to breathe. His Achilles could be felt, but he pushed it to the back of his mind.

Dan was encouraged all the way by one of the training team members, who had been with him from the

213

beginning. As he went over the footbridge towards the base, some off-duty Royal Marines screamed at him to keep going. He limped on through the main gates and down to the firing range. Dan had to shoot six out of ten bullets on target from 25-metres, simulating 200 metres with the rifle he carried throughout the test to pass. He shot all ten on target. The test was over. They all gathered anxiously in the grotts for the results. The whole troop had come in under 73 minutes which was brilliant. Individual times were then handed out; Dan had a few minutes to spare on his result, but it was nowhere near the times he had been getting before his injury.

The next day was Sunday. This would be the only day of rest before the other three Commando tests took place. Monday, the nine-mile speed march. Tuesday is the Tarzan assault course, and Wednesday is the final test which is the 30 miler.

Dan decided to stay on base while others ventured into Exeter for a change of scenery and respite from the pressure of what was to come.

Dan headed down to the social hub where he met a couple of lads that he knew that had recently passed the

Commando tests. The one that was preying on his mind was the 30 miler. This was because he had never done 30 miles before, and it was an unknown entity. The other three he had practised many times before and knew he could complete them given the right circumstances.

Never afraid to ask questions, whether it made him look stupid or not. Dan asked the lads how difficult it was. The answer was, as expected, very hard, both mentally and physically draining. Videos of it that Dan has seen depict a gentle stroll over the moors. The lads told him to expect the worst and double it, and he would be fine. With the knowledge of what was to come, Dan plugged for a takeaway and an early night.

Dan rang to say his day was dragging, and he just wanted these next three days over with. He said the tension in the grotts was steadily rising. All the lads had formed a close bond. Although Dan had not been in this particular troop long, they had all met before and had welcomed him into the troop with open arms.

Just twenty recruits left out of an original sixty-five. This will be the last troop to complete training under the original Royal Marine training regime. The new training plan would give the recruit the opportunity of invaluable training over a four-week period at Lympstone rather than the PRMC (three-day training plan). They then will take a test to see if they have the makings of a Royal Marine. Upon passing, the thirty-two weeks of training will begin.

The torment for Jon and I began again. I hadn't slept particularly well but felt full of energy. It was the day of the nine-mile speed march. This is a combination of running and marching. Dan said they would be aiming for ten-minute miles or under, carrying a complete fighting order. This means webbing, which fits around the waist and a rifle and weighs in total approximately 32lbs. The PT instructor will set the pace, and as they all knew full well, it would undoubtedly be eight to nine-minute miles.

As we waited once more for news, we grew more anxious. Dan eventually rang to say they had all completed the test in under the ninety minutes allocated. Jon and I could breathe once more.

A drummer from the Royal Marines band met them at the end of the run, near the entrance to Lympstone.

The troop then marched behind the drummer through the training camp. They saluted the company sergeant major as they marched past. Serving marines, personnel, and Nods clap them as they pass by. Dan's previous sergeant from the Netherlands and some of his old training team have taken a break from their duties to clap Dan in. Dan said he felt so proud of the troop and realised his dream could potentially become a reality very soon. Two down, two to go, and the worst yet to come.

On the Tuesday morning, Dan set his alarm for 5.30 am. Shower, then across to the galley for breakfast. The lads were in good spirits, ready to take on the next challenge. Dan said the atmosphere was lighter, and laughter could be heard around the grotts. The Tarzan assault course is very deceiving, and many recruits have got it wrong and suffered injuries that knocked them back in training for several months. So it's not to be taken for granted. Dan likes this course because it is fast and he is very agile. The course itself has a time limit of 13 minutes and must be completed in that time. Testing is conducted while carrying 32 pounds of equipment and a rifle. The first part is an aerial confidence test which involves seven different obstacles, including zip wires and ropes which are positioned high up in the treetops. The troops run on to the assault course they know all too well. They must overcome twelve obstacles, and it's finished off with a thirty-foot wall climb. This test requires courage and determination; carrying out the correct drills and skills is the key to success, as well as a high level of all-around cardiovascular fitness.

Dan rings to let us know he completed the test in good time and will spend the rest of the day rolling his muscles and preparing for the big one. One member of the troop failed due to losing his grip on the monkey bars. He will repeat the test on Friday and hopefully pass.

The final test loomed. The troop will leave today and stay overnight at a location close to the start of the 30 miler. The 30 miler begins at Okehampton battle camp at the top end of Dartmoor and finishes near Plymouth. Dan is dreading this one. He tells me he is in pain with his Achilles. It has had a battering these last few days. The painkillers he has been taking are no longer easing the pain as much. Dan is apprehensive about whether he will make it or not. Thirty miles is a long way with Achilles pain, and considering the Achilles tendon is probably the most crucial tendon you have when walking and running, my fears were he could damage it further to the point he would be off for months.

This was the one decision I could not make. Dan knew the risks involved in continuing with the 30 miler. As far as he was concerned, he had to try. If the pain got too much, Dan would stop, which was the end of the conversation. I knew he wouldn't stop. He would crawl on his hands and knees to complete this one last test if he had to.

I awoke early on Wednesday morning with a banging headache; an excellent start to the day, I thought, trying to brush aside last night's conversation. I felt my stomach churn as visions of Dan's suffering came to the forefront of my mind. The pain he must be carrying was unthinkable. I checked the weather report for the Dartmoor area. It had snowed overnight, and the next couple of days, there was widespread frost. The lady on the news finished off by saying it would be 'treacherous underfoot'.

I took Ellie out up to Wiswell and across the fields. The sun was just peeking over the hill tops, it was bitterly cold, but you could see it would be a beautiful bright day. I kept that thought in my head for later.

Ellie and I returned just in time to see Jon before he went to bed. He had been on the night shift and looked the way I felt. He gave me strict instructions to wake him if there was any news.

I spent most of the morning keeping occupied with work, answering emails, advertising vacancies, etc. All the while keeping my eye on the time and my mobile.

Janice tried to distract me on teams, talking about anything but Dan. Janice has been through the ups and downs with me. She listened and advised me when it mattered. Janice was also on tenterhooks hoping his dream would come true.

Once again, no news is good news. Jon got up at about 2.00 pm, no longer able to sleep. He popped his head around the office door, 'Any news?' he asks.

'None,' I replied.

We must just wait. Dan had said that they took their phones off them before the 30-miler, and he didn't know if they would get them back before returning to Lympstone.

I went downstairs to make a coffee. Texts were coming through thick and fast, asking if Dan had done it. I just couldn't reply to any of them. When I had news, I would let them know.

My phone once more pinged to let me know there was another message. I looked at my phone, and it was from Dan. My stomach dropped, and it took me right back to his first Final X and the message I had received then.

Another message came through from Dan; only this was a photo. I steadied myself expecting to see an image of my son in an ambulance or a hospital bed. Instead, it was a picture of my beautiful son wearing a green beret with a caption saying, 'I did it, Mum'. The last time he had said that was when he had passed his PRMC sixteen months ago. Tears began to fall. I called Jon and screamed, 'He did it.' Jon rushed in to find me in tears clutching the picture of our son with his green beret. Tears streamed down Jon's face in torrents. You could see the pride he had for his youngest son overspilling. He was absolutely made up.

Dan had shown such courage and determination from beginning to end.

Dan rang me minutes later. I think he couldn't quite believe his journey was complete. He said he had been given his green beret by an officer from the Special Boat Service. The officer ran with him for several miles. Dan had fallen behind early due to the pain in his foot. His painkillers hadn't yet kicked in, so he was in excruciating agony.

One of the training team members stuck to him like glue, continuously encouraging him. He fell several times on ruts of grass. The paths were uneven if you could call them paths. In some areas, he had to plough through gorse bushes and through streams, up banks and down steep inclines.

At the first checkpoint, Dan guzzled water and took another painkiller that seemed to kick in straight away. There were six checkpoints which included water stops and refuelling. He was ten minutes behind the rest of the troop. Dan could see his troop just heading over a ridge in the distance. He needed to up his game to complete the 30-miler in the time allocated, which was eight hours.

After the third checkpoint, he knew he was over halfway, and it was doable if he kept up the pace and could remain on his feet. Dan said he passed through a stage nearing the end of pure numbness. From his knee downwards, it was as if he was floating in the air. Whether it was his brain cutting out the pain or something else. It didn't matter. Due to his internal strength and wilfulness, he was able to rejoin his troop and keep pace. The end was in sight. Dan said he could feel the adrenalin kick in during the last four miles. The smiles began to form on the recruits' faces. Dan said you could feel everyone's excitement. They knew it was within their grasp. The training team kept pushing them along. Dan said he had looked at the PT instructor next to him, who had been right by his side all the way. A smirk came across his face, it was the middle of winter, minus five at the most, and the instructor next to him had a P.T. vest on and was running across Dartmoor with a cripple. You couldn't make it up. All the pain was nearly over. Dan's legs were on auto-pilot; he dreaded the pain he would feel when he eventually came to a stop. Dan started to imagine life beyond training in the last hour of running. They were about to join the most exclusive club in the world. Had it been worth all the pain and heartache? Without a doubt. Yes. Yes. Yes.

Within their sight was the famous bridge. Sadly, there was no one to clap them in. Tourists would usually wait by the bridge to congratulate the recruits on their performance. Because of Covid 19 and the restrictions in effect, the bridge was empty.

The troop came over the bridge knowing they had all completed all their commando tests. They slowed to a stop. Dan admitted he felt overwhelmed and tearful, knowing they had completed the four commando tests and were about to be awarded the green beret. They congratulated each other then proceeded to walk the short distance to 42 Commando for the presentation of the coveted green beret.

The troop lined up to receive their green berets. When it came to Dan, the high-ranking officer said he admired Dan for the sheer grit and determination he had shown for such a young lad. He also commented that he wouldn't have been able to complete the 30-miler at seventeen years of age. The whole troop had completed the 30-miler. Unfortunately, the lad who had failed the Tarzan assault course the day before did not receive his green beret as he had not completed all the tests. It must have been a sickening experience for the young lad. I suppose it would spur him on to complete it on Friday. The lads in the troop rallied around him and made light of the situation and soon had him laughing as he was the only nod left in the troop.

They headed back to Lympstone. All of them were exhausted yet feeling elated from the whole experience. Dan said it felt like having a weight lifted from you.

They arrived back at camp. Having been sat on the coach for some time, it was a struggle to walk to the grotts. Their bodies were aching. Some had injuries that were so painful. Dan was in pain from his Achilles. He took some more painkillers, which eased the pain considerably. As his body relaxed, he had aches all over and knew he would suffer in the morning if he didn't use the roller. Thus, despite being exhausted, he rolled his muscles to limit tomorrow's pain.

Friday morning arrived. Despite the pain he was still in, Dan was up early. He knew that one of the troop members must retake the Tarzan assault course. Dan was aware that the retest would begin soon; he sneaked out and wandered down to the bottom field. An old sweatshirt under his arm was be used to wipe the morning dew off the monkey bars. This will ensure that the recruit from his troop will have a better grip when he gets to them during the test. Fingers crossed, this small act of kindness will work, and he will receive his green beret this morning.

The boys from the troop walk down to the bottom field when the test is due to take place. It was like watching a group of elderly men out for an afternoon stroll, Dan said. Several members of the troop have been experiencing aches and pains after the last few weeks. The lad in question had passed the other three commando tests. He just needed to pass this one, and he will be joining his chosen Commando unit.

They caught a glimpse of him running down to the bottom field. They started shouting and urging him on. Once he approached the monkey bars, not a sound can be heard. He grabs the first bar, the second, the third, and before he knew it, he was over them and onto the next obstacle. The lads are willing him on once more. Now for the thirty-foot wall and up he goes. The stopwatch was pressed, and they all waited with bated breath for the result. He had passed. They all ran over and congratulated him on his achievement.

Dan said it took real courage to complete the 30-miler knowing he had failed the Tarzan assault course earlier in the week. The troop had worked as a team and kept each other motivated through odd comments of encouragement. They crossed the line together with one common goal. To become a Royal Marine Commando.

PASSING OUT

Having watched the young lad from his troop being presented with his beret by the Sergeant Major, they had all returned back to the grotts. Dan said he felt like he had been hit by a juggernaut, so he opted to crawl back into bed for a while. Later he opened his eyes and remembered what had happened a couple of days before, and a huge grin spread across his face. The pain he felt in his limbs would pass. However, the feeling of accomplishing his dream, he hoped, would stay with him for a long time to come, if not forever.

Dan and the rest of the troop were to train for the next seven days; they would pass out the following week. After Covid 19, the excitement that would usually surround this particular day has diminished. Parents and friends were not allowed on the base for obvious reasons. However, we would be sent a link to watch the passing out, which was kindly arranged by the Royal Marines Charity.

Normally guests would arrive in all their finery, watch their relative receive their green beret followed by a celebration meal—a superb day by all accounts.

So the troop must continue to keep the tradition of the passing out process, which means hours on the parade ground practising drill. This is part of the job most Marines hate. They are taught drill at the beginning of training and pick it up again at the end of training. They start at eight in the morning and finish when the drill sergeant is happy with their progress.

Dan rings when his day is over. He received his posting this morning. Dan was lucky enough to get his first choice. He is over the moon. Another ten lads from his troop are also heading to the same company.

As a result of Dan's Achilles pain, the doctor has recommended that he wear trainers while doing drill practice. This would ease the pressure of wearing the heavy black boots they use on the parade ground. He would hopefully be able to stand tall among the rest of the troop on pass-out day.

Jon and I received the link so we could watch, live, Dan's pass out. Jon and I were glued to the live stream at 11.00 am on the 12th of February 2021.

Dan rang the night before. He said the troop were all looking forward to the following day, although it would have been far better if the families had been there, it was better than nothing. His blues were ready, and his boots were polished to within an inch of their life.

Friday morning arrived. I woke early and spent a while thinking about the journey we had all been on. I thought about how I would feel. This was the day our son would pass out and officially be a Royal Marine Commando.

I felt the relief of our son accomplishing his dream. That is what he set out to do, and that is what he has done, which is incredible. For Jon and me, the pain and worry will continue as it will with any other person's child. We never stop worrying. That is part of being a parent.

While writing this, tears are rolling down my face because I know he has chosen a high-risk career path within the military. I also know if anything terrible happened to him, we would take great comfort in the fact he died serving in the Corps and doing what he loved to do more than anything. Not many people can say that.

Some may say it is a bit morbid to think that way. Being realistic would be my assessment. When we signed the paperwork to allow Dan to become a recruit, it dawned on us what may happen. From that day, we started to live with it. Sixteen months on, we have come to terms with this fact, and we will continue to live with it and support him all we can. Dan is well aware of the risks, and he knows he has our full support.

The morning flew by quickly, and before I knew it, it was 10.45 am. We had received lots of messages wishing Dan well and congratulating him on his achievement.

We were still in lockdown in the northwest. So we could not share this moment with other people in our house. We settled down to watch this monumental occasion on our own. The troop came marching into the indoor parade square to the sound of the Royal Marine band. I was scanning the screen in the hope of catching my first glimpse of Dan in his blues. There were three rows of troops. Dan was in the second row. He looked so smart. I could feel myself welling up. He had transformed from a boy to a man in what seemed like overnight. The Royal Marines band was playing, and the troop was standing to attention. It was incredible to see everything synchronised to perfection. A high-ranking officer spoke to each member of the troop individually, congratulating them on their achievement.

He then turned his attention to the friends and family watching from home. He pointed out that we had now joined the family and thanked us for our support, which I thought was really nice. He also spoke about the role of the Corps and how that was about to change. The padre then said a few words, and then a call rang out on the parade ground from the commanding officer, 'Royal Marines To Your Duties.' The band struck up and started to play 'A Life on the Ocean Wave.' The troop marched off the parade square to much applause, closely followed by the Royal Marine Band.

The day was over for us but not for the troop. The screen turned black, and the moment we had dreamed about for sixteen months had disappeared in a flash. The texts kept pouring in from friends and family who had also watched it from the comfort of their homes.

They would enjoy their pass-out in true commando style, and what happens at the pass-out party nobody apart from the participants really know. Or should I say nobody wants to know?

The following day there are a few sore heads, including Dan's. Unfortunately, they had not been able to celebrate as many troops had done in the past. They were still not allowed off camp, so they have made the most of it on camp.

They could sit back and relax for a few days and enjoy what time they had left together as a troop.

COMING HOME

Due to the lift in restrictions with COVID 19, the troop were allowed to go home for a long weekend before going to their designated troop or taking up their driving lessons.

Jon picked Dan up after work. I arranged for the neighbours to have a celebratory drink on the street when he arrived home, which he was not expecting. Jon asked Dan to let me know they were close. Dan, obviously, did not know what was in store for him. The car came down the road, and everybody let out a rip-roaring cheer. The look on Dan's face was a picture. He climbed out of the car and thanked everybody for the rapturous applause.

Individual neighbours congratulated him on his success. Soon the conversation turned to the adventures he had already had and what was to come. For once, he was enjoying the limelight and soaked up the praise he received.

Jon and I thanked everybody for taking the time to make Dan's homecoming special. Slowly, the street turned into an empty road once more. Dan looked washed out and is still limping. He says his Achilles is healing, but it will take time.

Dan took all his gear upstairs and reappeared with a plastic bag. He told us to sit down. Jon and I sat down, not really sure what to expect.

Dan began to tell us about the many traditions the Royal Marines adhere to. One of them is a green beret, which must be given to the mother of a Royal Marine. The Corps seem to think we had earned it, and I must admit I think I have too. A beautiful gesture. The beret is lined with silk, and it went into my keepsake box.

The leather-bound dagger is no less a keepsake for the father of a Royal Marine. Jon was absolutely made up. He has pictures of his passing out and of his troop. The rest of the evening was spent listening to what they got up to during pass out.

Now I am not so sure this is a tradition. However, before they marched onto the parade ground on pass-out day, they each had a tot of Navy Rum or two to keep the cold out. In my eyes, they earned it, illegal or not

Dan's three-day leave was spent firstly with Cameron's family, who desperately wanted to congratulate him on his success. We then had a meal for him at home as the restaurants were still closed due to Covid.

The time came all too soon for Dan to return to Lympstone. He seemed much happier now that the weight had been lifted from his shoulders. His bags were packed, and he was ready to depart. He gives me the usual bear hug and starts heading for the door. He turns and says. 'I love you, Mum.' And the door shuts once more.

Tears made their usual journey down my face. My stomach churned. I will never be able to stop myself from crying when he has to leave for as long as I live. It is so painful. Just a Mum thing, I suppose.

The troop soon moved out of their grotts and took up residence in the trained ranks accommodation, which by all accounts is a little bit more palatial. Their old accommodation was thoroughly cleaned until it gleamed.

Things started to change straight away. One of the corporals went in to see the lads in Dan's room. He asked them to call him by his first name in future, shook each of their hands individually, and left them stunned.

The Royal Marines are undergoing huge changes. As part of the transformation, they were all issued with new uniforms. Instead of the multi-terrain pattern, the new uniform features a multi-cam pattern. Crye Precision has produced the multi-cam, a camouflage pattern that can be used in a variety of environments. When Dan was informed that his new uniform was in the stores, it was like all his Christmases had come at once. He face-timed Jon and me, and we had a sort of military fashion show. Everything fit perfectly, and he looked so smart.

Dan also noticed a massive change in the galley. They no longer have to sit in the canteen area. They can sit in the trained ranks area. Seemingly, the food has stepped up a notch or two as well—omelettes to order no less. The downside is he now has to pay for it.

With his brand new uniform on and his perfectly shaped green beret, he looked over to the Nod area of the canteen. He could see the pain in their eyes as they tried to force down as much food as possible to keep them energised. Not knowing what torturous exercise was coming next. Dan remembered looking over to where he was now sat, wondering if things do get better. The answer to that is yes without a doubt. He finished his lunch and headed outside.

There are a troop of Nods heading his way. The Nods will be uncertain of his rank, so they saluted him as he passed to save themselves a dressing down. He calls out, 'At ease, lads.' The troop carried on with their day. Dan chuckled to himself. He could not believe what had just happened. He has just had lads in their twenties saluting him—a seventeen-year-old who is now a trained rank no less. The sergeant from the Netherlands came to find him to say he was returning home. Dan thanked him for everything he taught him and wished him well. As he explained it to me on the phone, I knew he would miss him; he would never be able to thank him enough for all the support and encouragement he had given him. Dan finished off by explaining that in time he aspired to be like him.

Within the next week, quite a few of the boys from Dan's troop transferred to their new units. Dan stayed with a few others at Lympstone to complete his driving tests. Yes, I said tests.

Dan would firstly complete his driving test. He then moved up to a twenty-ton truck. On passing that test, he moved up to a forty-ton truck. He completed all these tests before he was eighteen. He had never even had the pleasure of driving a car. I am not sure whether that is a positive or negative thing. I must admit I am so grateful to the military for saving me all the stress and worry that is associated with driving lessons.

Dan was quite excited about his driving lessons. Anything new that taxed his brain is good for Dan. They would be driving for three hours a day, and he was booked in from eight until eleven in the morning, with a pitstop for breakfast in between. Tuesday was his first lesson. My mobile started to ring not long after 2.00 pm. It was Dan. He said he could not believe how stressful it was and how you were supposed to accomplish everything while keeping your eyes on the road. I reassured him it would fall into place

The driving instructor, Roger, had taken him to a quiet road on a residential estate to practice the basics. Dan mastered the clutch bite quickly, and after three days, Roger said he was ready to take the highways and byways of Devon after the weekend. Dan wasn't that sure.

Roger was a very quiet chap, only spoke when it was necessary. Dan said all he ever commented on was, 'Keep checking your mirrors,' I suppose it was better than someone constantly chattering and interrupting your concentration. Each day started with driving, then admin and then cleaning of the grotts.

The other thing about being a trained rank was that you could leave the base when you were off duty. The remaining lads from the troop decided to walk down to the local farm shop. They sold fabulous fish and chips, and there was always room to sit outside and enjoy the remaining daylight hours.

On occasion, they would buy meat from the local butcher in the farm shop. They would then amble down to the beach in Exmouth for a barbecue until late in the evening. They were all enjoying their newfound freedom and spent many sun-drenched afternoons on the beach at Exmouth eyeing up the ladies. Life was slowly getting back to normal for them. They had not been able to go to Exmouth when they were Nods. They were told early on in training they were not allowed to venture in that direction. This is because most of the training teams spent evenings in Exmouth. It was not appropriate for the recruits to be there, especially when they had had a beer or two.

Monday came round once more, and driving had started to become enjoyable. Outside the gates, Roger would be waiting. Dan would climb into the driver's seat, and off they would go. When Dan rang in the evenings, he always had a tale to tell. By Thursday, Roger was confident Dan would be OK to sit his test the following Tuesday.

Dan woke early on Tuesday morning. Having spoken to him the night before, he was not at all worried in the least and was quite laid back about the whole thing.

I think after everything he had been through, a driving test was neither here nor there. He could take it again if he failed.

They arrived at the test centre in good time and waited patiently for the examiner to call his name. A tall gentleman approached him, quickly followed by another guy behind him. Apparently, the examiner is also being examined. So Dan set off with the two passengers watching his every move.

Dan arrived back at the test centre where Roger was waiting for him. Roger could see Dan chatting to the two men before they left the vehicle.

Big smiles from Dan. He passed his driving test the first time. Now for the twenty-ton truck.

Dan embraced the trucks. The guy who was teaching him was ex-military, so they were on the same wavelength and had the same kind of humour. Dan was a lot more relaxed and mastered the huge vehicle with ease. After just one week, he had passed his twenty-ton truck test. Now for the forty-ton truck.

His instructor Rob picked him up from the base, and they drove over to a disused airfield. For most of the morning, they practised reversing the forty-ton truck into allocated areas, coupling and uncoupling the trailer.

They then drove for fifty minutes in and around the Exeter area. They did this for about four days.

Within a week, Rob put Dan in for his test. The test started off well. The examiner has chosen one of the many country lanes that litter the Devon coastline. As they approached one of the small villages dotted around the area, he asked Dan to turn left. He is aware that he had to drive on the other side of the road to make the corner. As he attempted to move over, a car came down the hill towards the truck at speed. Dan pulled the truck back to avoid the vehicle and missed the turn. It was an automatic fail.

They headed back to the test centre, where Rob assured him it was not a problem. The following day they practised the turning procedure again. Even if the same situation cropped up again, he would be able to handle it this time. The next test he took, the lorry broke down on the dual carriageway. So that particular one was abandoned.

Third time lucky, they say. Upon his arrival at the disused airfield, Dan was examined on his reversing, coupling, and uncoupling of the trailer that makes up the

40-ton truck. He then once more drove the examiner for fifty minutes on the local A roads. The examiner then congratulated him on his pass.

They headed back to camp, where Rob shook Dan's hand and told him that it'd been a pleasure. Dan wished him well and returned to the grotts to pack up his remaining gear.

This was a monumental day. Not only has he passed all his driving tests. His training at Lympstone is officially over. It has been an arduous journey, filled with highs and lows. He arrived at Lympstone as a young, naive boy and left a man. Dan has learned so much, not just how to be a competent Royal Marine, but how to be a decent person too. He has had the most inspiring role models he could have wished for and took away with him the knowledge that dreams do come true. If you put the effort in, you can and will achieve.

Jon set off on the six-hour journey to bring his son home. He will have to pack everything up, from his Bergen to the laundry bag, and bring it home. We would then sort everything out from here.

I could not believe Dan would be home for his eighteenth birthday. The cake was ordered, and the meal was booked. I had also arranged a party for the following Saturday with all his friends. We have not been able to congratulate him properly, so it was the ideal opportunity before he moved to his new unit. I will not bore you with the details, but it was one hell of a party!!!

This is where my diary ends. Everything that has happened over the last eighteen months, from cracked ribs to Covid 19, has been written down. I will continue to log my son's story and the adventures he will no doubt have. I will keep them, so when the time comes, Daniel will be able to share his adventures with his children one day. Only this time, they will be real.

Words will never convey how proud we are of this young man. We have all shared his journey from the postman to the pet food supplier. We have all felt his pain and his happiness. Jon and I have been overwhelmed with the support we have received from friends and family. You have all made our journey so much easier, and I know our son has appreciated your words of encouragement.

As he embarks on the next part of his journey Jon and I will continue to support and love the boy who defied all the odds.

A Note from the Author

Our son has been strong enough to face his nemesis and beat the doubters to call himself a Royal Marine Commando. This book is written from a diary I kept of his journey. Some people may say it's no big deal.

A sixteen-year-old leaves home. Leaves all he has ever known to follow a dream. To become a lifelong member of one of the world's most elite fighting forces. I am only his Mum and probably slightly biased, but yes, I think it's a big deal.

It would be wonderful if this book could somehow shape and inspire another young person's life and impart optimism in their efforts to overcome the largest hurdles and dream big. This book will then have been worth writing.

For mothers out there that feel they need to hold on to their child a little longer. Don't. Allow them to fly. Let them follow their dreams, large or small. The biggest reason we don't follow our dreams is the thought of failure. This is, in my opinion, not a good enough excuse not to try. Failure is part of the learning process and should be welcomed, not feared.

I do not class myself as an academic or an author. I have put pen to paper in my darkest hours and have written from the heart. In turn, this has brought positivity to my life, which everybody needs.

I know that by completing this journey with my son, I am a better person. Things for me are no longer black and white. There are grey areas to be negotiated, which Janice, my boss, will be thankful for.

I also realised how kind people can be. All the support Jon and I have had, from Rob and Emma at Harris Fitness to the pet shop supplier. All the neighbours with their words of encouragement when he came home on leave. This all meant a lot to us.

The biggest thanks of all go to my work colleagues who have stood by me through thick and thin.

They have encouraged me through the darkest of days and held my hand when needed.

We thank you all for your support.

Printed in Great Britain
by Amazon

78713536R00144